Also by Diana Alishouse

Depression Visible: the Ragged Edge

Farm Wife Stories
a Memoir

Diana Alishouse

My Own Ship Press

Farm Wife Stories: a Memoir
© 2022 Diana Alishouse

ISBNL (print)   978-1-951368-46-3
ISBN: (e-book)   978-1-951368-29-6

Published by
My Own Ship Press
PO Box 490153
Lawrenceville GA 30049

To Marvin,
the love of my life
(even though he was
cantankerous sometimes)

How We Got Together – Denver – September 1981

MY NEW NEXT-DOOR neighbors greeted me across the back fence. We talked about gardening, the neighborhood, where we were from, and all the usual chitchat. The wife, Ilene, finally asked if I was married.

"Well, yes," I told her. "But not for long. The divorce will be final next month, and I can hardly wait."

Without a pause, the man, Walter, said, "You'll have to meet my brother Marvin. He's divorced too."

Yeah, right, I thought. *I'm no good at this marriage stuff. Two times is enough for me.*

I smiled nicely and made an excuse to go inside.

A few weeks later I came home from work on a Friday and spotted a rather grizzled cowboy clad in jeans, western shirt, boots, and well-worn cowboy hat sitting on the raised planter in Walter and Ilene's front yard. "Aren't they home?" I asked.

"No, but they'll be here soon." He had a new-looking blue truck parked at the curb. I noticed there wasn't a lot of chrome.

I'd been planning to have a garage sale that weekend, so I changed clothes and started making tables with sawhorses and plywood. The cowboy came over to help.

"Where do you want this table?" he asked.

"Here," I said. "The other two go over there. Be sure to leave room between them."

My daughter came outside. I introduced the two of them and asked her to start bringing out the boxes of sale items. Marvin didn't talk much—just asked if he could help with the boxes. Eventually we put tarps over the tables for the night. I thanked him, and he went back to his brother's house.

He came to the sale on Saturday and again on Sunday, making himself useful carrying things to buyers' cars, keeping an eye on everything—especially the cash box—and joining the conversations among shoppers and my many neighbors who dropped in.

At one point during a lull in activity on Sunday afternoon we were standing side by side. Without thinking I slipped my hand into his. It felt good. It was probably his Stetson cologne that made me do it.

A few weeks later he came to visit his brother and sister-in-law again. When I came home from work he was sitting on the planter, but he sauntered into my driveway as I got out of the car.

"Would you like to go to supper this evening?"

Supper. Not dinner. Farm boy for sure.

"And maybe," he added, "we could go dancing, if you know a good place."

"Well. There's a place near here called The Urban Cowboy." Neither of my previous husbands had been able to dance. It was something I missed.

Dinner was fine. He was kind of shy. We talked a little about our previous spouses, children, my job at a graphic design business, and his farm in eastern Colorado where he raised wheat and cattle.

When we reached The Urban Cowboy, the place was packed with people younger than the two of us and all dressed up in citified cowboy attire—brand new with lots of fringe, flimsy hats, and boots that had never felt dirt.

Marvin grabbed my hand, told me to stay behind him and hold onto his belt. He slowly walked into the crowd. To my astonishment, the conversational noise level dropped, and they parted like the Red Sea for Moses. Every cowboy-wannabe in there recognized the real thing when they saw it. Presence—he had gobs of it.

He stopped at the dance floor, turned, took me in his arms, and we began to dance. He was strong. My left hand on his shoulder felt the dense muscles made by days and years of hard physical work, not at all like the city dudes who went to the gym to work out once or twice a week. This man was solid. And he knew how to dance!

Fuel Stop in the City – Denver – October 1981

"**WE NEED FUEL**," Marvin said and pulled into a gas station.

"Um…" I'd noticed the NO TRUCKS sign at the pump where he stopped.

"Um, what?"

"See that sign?"

"This isn't a truck. It's a pickup."

"But this is a city, and a pickup is considered a truck here."

In his well-worn cowboy clothes and with complete self-confidence, he got out and began running diesel fuel into his truck—or pickup, or whatever.

Though the employees inside the station stood at the window and stared at him, they made no comment when he went inside to pay.

Not Farm Material

AFTER MARVIN HAD made several trips to see me, he brought his widowed mother along. They both stayed with Walter and Ilene, but the next day, a Sunday, he came over to see if I wanted to join them for dinner, which I found out meant lunch. They ate chicken-fried steak with mashed potatoes and gravy. I ate salad.

His mother, a short round lady, mostly ignored me as the three of them talked about crops and cows and the farm. I learned that it took ten acres to support one cow and that Marvin ran "pairs."

"Pairs of what?" I asked.

"Cow-calf pairs."

"Oh.

Much later I learned that when he asked his mother that evening what she thought of me, she told him, "She seems okay, but I don't think she's farm material."

Into the Wilderness – Eastern Colorado – November 1981

BY THIS TIME, we were talking on the phone a lot. One evening he asked if he could pick me up and take me to the farm for the weekend. My daughter was going to be with her dad, so I gulped and said okay.

"Can Cindy come, too," I asked.

"Sure."

What am I getting into? I wondered.

On Friday, I managed to get off work an hour early, so I waited nervously for him to arrive. Sure enough—there he was, calmly walking up to my door and ringing the bell. I swallowed hard.

"You ready?"

"Sure." I didn't have even the slightest tremor in my voice.

He picked up my overnight bag; I picked up Cindy's leash; the three of us climbed into his pickup.

I sat in the middle close to him, smelling the subtle drift of his Stetson cologne. Cindy, my Samoyed, sat between me and the door. After a little while she whined and pawed at me, then walked across my lap, squirmed her way next to Marvin, gently pushing me out of her way, did her *three-times-around-circle*, settled between us, and went to sleep.

"What was that about?"

"I don't know. She's never done that before. Maybe she didn't feel secure being next to the door."

"Or maybe she didn't like you sitting so close to me."

I thought about that for a while. "No," I said. "I think she's telling me you're a trustworthy person. Dogs can sense things people can't. I've had several dogs, and I've learned to respect their knowledge and their opinions about people."

"Hmmm," said Marvin.

"I remember one evening when I was alone in my store in Steamboat Springs. It was pretty dark outside, and I was getting ready to close for the day when two men came in. They stood for a few seconds looking around. One of them took a step toward me, and Cindy, who had been standing beside me, took one step toward him—no growling, just an attitude of alertness. And the hair on the back of her neck stood up just a trifle. The men turned around and left. I think she saved me from being robbed or worse."

"Hmmm," Marvin repeated.

In spite of Cindy's calm presence, the 100-mile drive from Denver to his farm got scarier the farther we went. First we were on Interstate 70. Then we turned onto a two-lane state highway, and by this time it was well into the evening. When we passed a sign announcing that we were entering another county. Marvin said, "Whenever I get here, I figure I'm almost home."

Good, I thought. *Only another mile or two.* The next time we turned—this time onto a narrow bumpy two-lane country road—it was getting downright dark.

What am I getting into? I wondered yet again.

Cindy was still asleep between the two of us. After driving what seemed like an eternity, we turned onto another dirt road—the kind with three ruts worn into it. The middle rut holds the wheels on the driver's side, since only one car would fit comfortably on the road at a time.

By this time it was truly dark. No moon. A few yard-lights miles apart. *Jeez. What now?*

Soon he turned onto yet another farm road. "See that light ahead? We're nearly there."

Yes, there was a light—a dim light—but it gradually grew larger, and he finally pulled into the driveway. All I could see was the bright circle cast by the yard light.

His house was nothing wonderful, and it was plain there hadn't been a woman looking after it. Cindy sniffed her way around the house thoroughly, then came back to me and wagged her tail.

He'd told me to bring warm clothes, so I was prepared with jeans, turtlenecks, sweaters, a parka, and boots. After all, I used to live in the high Rockies. I knew how to stay warm.

The next morning he came strolling out of the bedroom in dark green coveralls over his regular clothes. He had a hat with earflaps and a visor. So much for the dashing cowboy appearance. The November wind was biting. I wished I had clothes like his. I vowed next time I would bring my long underwear. Even then I knew there would be a next time.

We toured the farm—starting with the fields. He told me about each one: the *Section*, the *200*, the *100*, *Virginia's Quarter*, and *Over the Hill*. The school section, he explained, was 640 acres that was technically owned by the state. Farmers who had sections rented them and the rent money went to support the school system. It cost more to rent crop sections than the pasture sections that some farmers had.

When I thought all that part was done, he showed me more: the *Old Alfalfa Patch* with an adjoining one hundred acres that seemed to have no name, the *Two Fields South of the House*, the one *Next to the Pasture on the Other Side of the Road*. They all looked pretty much the same to me. All I could see was rolling land, obviously cultivated fields, some with stubble, some that looked like little rows of grass dormant for the winter. I learned that those were the fields that had been sown in September and would be ready for harvest in July.

There was little color in the landscape. The only trees were elms, forlorn and barren, guarding the distant homesteads. I learned later that the pioneers had brought eastern trees west with them to this vast prairie. I saw majesty in the textures of the landscape, and the smooth arc of the sky with its invisible winds.

"Does the wind always blow here?" I asked. I had lived in Boulder, Colorado, for a few years where I finally had wooden shutters installed on the west side of my house because of the terrible windstorms in late fall and early winter. I didn't want to live anywhere with winds that fierce.

"No," he told me. "We generally get a nice breeze in the summer."

The pasture was surrounded by a barbed wire fence. There were two barns—the old milk barn with no milk cows and the horse barn with no horses. Around the horse barn were some corrals. All of this was about a hundred feet from the house.

We drove into town for lunch at The Hearty Rancher, the kind of small-town place where everyone looks up to see who just walked in. They all greeted Marvin with either a curt nod or a question about his new hired man. He just said, "Nothing yet."

On the way back to the farm he explained how addresses had worked in the country before they had road signs. "Our place was eleven south, five and a half east, and a half south. Now we have a regular street address on Road JJ."

"Eleven south of what?"

"Eleven miles south of town." He sounded like that was the most logical explanation in the world. I guess it was.

"Oh," was all I could think to say.

All the roads went north and south or east and west. I still had no idea which fields were his.

Wheat in the Round-Top – November 1981

THE NEXT DAY we toured the rest of the buildings starting with the shop, a steel building eighty feet long with massive sliding doors on each end. My first glimpse of the wonders inside as he pushed one door open was of a monstrous red tractor—not at all like the ones I had played on as a child on my grandfather's farm in Mississippi.

This one had four sets of tires taller than I, and I had to climb a ladder to get into the enclosed cab. Marvin told me the machine was articulated. "Move the steering wheel a little and look out back," he said. I did and saw the tractor bend in the middle. "The front wheels don't turn," Marvin explained. "It's the back wheels that steer."

He told me a lot more about the tractor—make, model, and a lot of stuff I couldn't comprehend at that time. Little did I know how much I would learn in the future. I clambered happily around on his grain trucks and the combine as he continued to explain features and functions.

We inspected his workbench and tools, including wrenches way bigger than any I had ever seen and a drill press that put to shame the puny one I had used making silver jewelry. And he used a welder, a real welder, not the tiny acetylene soldering tips I had used.

Outside I'd noticed the row of round bins with conical tops. "Wheat storage," he said and proceeded to a long Quonset hut. That's what I called it because that's what I'd learned while growing up on Air Force bases where my father was stationed. "We call it the round-top," he said. "Here, I'll show you what's inside." He slid one of the huge doors aside.

"Oh, God," I said—not as profanity but in awe. The interior reminded me of the great Gothic cathedrals with glowing stained-glass windows I'd seen in Germany as a child. In this utilitarian building the light coming in through translucent panels near the top of the curving edifice shone softly on wheat—tons of wheat in a huge pile with a heavenly smell.

Getting Serious – December 1981 to March 1982

WE CONTINUED TO see each other and included our children—who ranged in age from twelve to twenty-four—in meals and outings both in Denver and at the farm.

Two of his children were already adults. His daughter Tamra was a freshman in college, and his eldest son had a wife and two children. My daughter Erica was fourteen, and Marvin's son Scott was twelve, so they were the ones we were most concerned about.

Marvin and Scott visited us one weekend. We played with my dog Cindy, told stories about happenings in our lives, went to a movie, and enjoyed hanging out. I found out later that as Marvin and Scott were going back home, Scott said, "Dad, we need a dog."

Marvin's reply was, "Yep. I have a plan."

Erica, Cindy, and I visited the farm the next weekend. While Scott and Erica climbed to the top of the wheat pile in the round-top, Cindy discovered an old motor in a corner. It was covered with dust and chaff, but Cindy knew there was something—a bug or a mouse or something—living in it. She sat transfixed in front of it—sniffing, staring at it, cocking her head, listening with both her ears straight up.

When Scott and Erica came rolling back down, they were filthy dirty and covered with chaff. Marvin handed each of them a scoop shovel and calmly told them to scoop the grain they'd dislodged back onto the pile. I was surprised when Erica eagerly complied. For several years I'd been struggling with her teenage contrariness whenever I asked her to do something. When they finished, Marvin said, "Well, now you've played in the wheat once, so you don't have to do it again." Then he took them to the shop and cleaned them off with his air hose. *What a wonderful tool to have,* I thought.

We made popcorn in the microwave, drove a mile or so into the pasture to check the windmill that pumped water for the cows, and generally had fun. As Erica and I headed home on Sunday, she said, "Mom, we need a microwave."

"Yeah," I replied. "I have a plan."

The next time Marvin and Scott came to visit, he brought an employment application. That man thinks of everything. After I filled it out and turned it in, we both had a good chuckle as I asked him the same questions.

Once he'd answered them suitably, we decided the best thing to do would be to get married. Marvin was forty-four. I was thirty-eight.

I designed our wedding invitations: an ink drawing of a stalk of wheat and an artist's paintbrush on the front, with all the *who, what, when,* and *where* on the inside. We invited my friends from Denver and relatives from Colorado Springs and Vermont, and Marvin's friends and relatives, all local. We decided to have the wedding at the farmhouse.

I resigned from my job as a bookkeeper/graphic designer by telling my boss I was taking a new position as Domestic Operations Manager of the Bar JA Ranch.

Then I packed up our belongings.

About a week before the wedding, Marvin, who knew full well the amount of stuff I had in my house, arrived with his stock trailer—yes, a stock trailer, the kind you put cows in. He had hosed it down and gotten most of the manure scrubbed out of the wooden floorboards. As we were

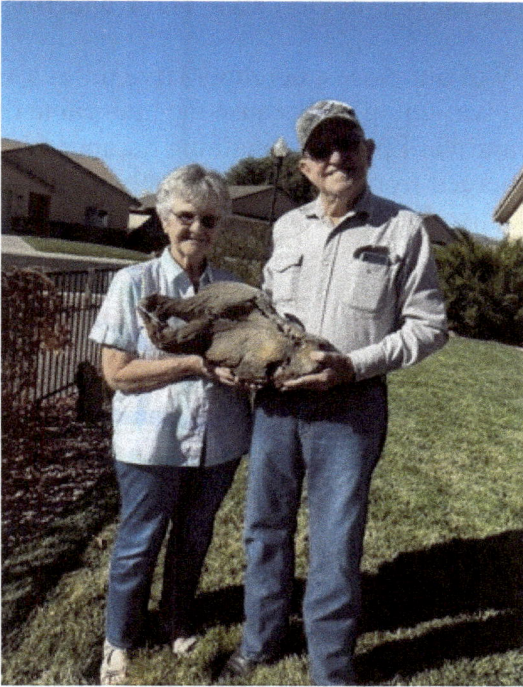

loading my stuff, I walked out the door with a box and found Marvin holding in his arms my most treasured piece of driftwood. He looked up at me and deadpanned, "I always wanted one of these." I laughed so hard I nearly dropped the box I was carrying.

Forty years later, I still have both those treasures—the man and the driftwood.

So away we moved to the farm where I:
- furiously cleaned house and integrated our furnishings and other belongings,
- planned food for the reception and all the people who would be spending the night after the wedding, and
- drafted a diagram of the house and yard showing sleeping arrangements for those who would be in the house and parking arrangements for those who were bringing their campers.

~ ~ ~

THE BIG DAY dawned. Marvin's oldest sister arrived with the beautiful wedding cake she had created. When she asked me where to put it, I burst into tears and wailed, "I don't know." My new big sister said, "Oh you poor thing. You've moved and gotten ready for a wedding with no bridesmaids to help." Then she took over, rearranging a few things and placing the cake. I've loved her ever since.

The preacher appeared and stood in front of the table. Erica escorted the groom from the back of the house and Scott escorted me from the front of the house. The service began, and just before the *I do* part, Cindy walked out from beneath the table where she'd been asleep and looked around at everybody, as if she were wondering where we'd all come from and what was going on. The whole room erupted in laughter. When calm returned, the ceremony continued without further disruption.

During the reception, several of the young women, led by Marvin's daughter Tamra, decided to kidnap the groom. They picked him up and stuffed him in the back seat of someone's car. My new step-daughter told me I'd have to pay a ransom to get him back. She handed me a paper bag and told me the ransom was seventeen cow-pies—dry enough to hold their shape and wet enough that they would shatter if dropped on the ground. They drove off into the wilds of eastern Colorado with Marvin grinning from the backseat.

A chilly March wind was blowing. My best friend from Denver and I jumped into her car and set off in pursuit, stopping in the middle of the road whenever we spotted cow-pies in a pasture beside the road. Have I mentioned the barbed-wire fences that enclosed all the pastures?

As Stephanie held the wires apart, I hiked the skirt of my wedding dress up as far as I could, wedged my feet deeper into my open-toed shoes, and eased as delicately as possible between two strands of barbed wire fencing. There I was, hair blowing across my face, trying not to step on the cow-pies, trying to find the right ones—not too wet, not too dry—and wondering what the hell kind of family had I gotten myself into.

We made several stops. One was in the driveway of our closest neighbor (five miles away from our house). Evidently they'd been notified of what was going on because the man came out and opened the gate to his pasture. What a hero! What a trove! I put the remaining number of pies needed into the sack just as the getaway vehicle emerged from behind the neighbor's house. The perpetrators tested the cow-pies rigorously. Apparently all seventeen passed the test, so they returned my husband to me.

And back we went to the party.

Getting Down to Business

THE DAY AFTER our wedding Marvin handed me his checkbook. "You know how to do bookkeeping," he said, "so from now on you can take care of this."

I opened it and stared at the check register. The blank check register. But I could see that fully half of the checks had already been used.

"How do you know how much money is in here?"

"I just remember what I've written checks for, and sometimes I look at the statement when it comes in. It's right on the mark, mostly."

I couldn't believe what I was hearing. "You remember all that?"

"Yeah, pretty much. I think about it a lot when I'm on the tractor."

I stared at him and thought hard. "This must be your personal checkbook. Do you also want me to take care of the farming business checkbook and accounting?"

"Oh, it's all in the one checking account."

Now I was totally dumbfounded. I had owned a few small businesses over the years and had worked as a bookkeeper for other businesses. I knew that personal and business revenues and expenses had to be kept separate.

What about inventories? I wondered. *How does he know how much wheat he has? He has to know that so he can account for the cost of goods sold. Oh, boy, am I in for a learning experience—this is going to be a monumental job.*

I was used to accrual accounting where an expense, such as for seed, would not be recognized when the seed was paid for, but would be tallied in when the resulting wheat crop was sold, thus matching the cost of producing the wheat to the revenue eventually received.

"Who does your taxes?" April 15th was fast approaching. How would I get things figured out before then? "Can we go meet with your tax preparer?"

"Sure. We'll go tomorrow." He paused. "We can see Bill after we get Erica enrolled in school." He paused again. "But the taxes this year have already been paid. I sent them in February."

I pondered this revelation. *Is he talking about quarterly estimated tax payments?* This didn't seem right, so I gave up. "Okay. Tomorrow."

~~~

ERICA WAS UNDERSTANDABLY nervous about going to a new school, but the principal and some of the teachers greeted us by name. *How do they know?* I wondered. I was slowly beginning to learn that small towns have intricate flows of information. *Probably everyone in town already knows everything there is to know about us.* I decided not to think of it as gossip. Marvin and Scott chatted with the principal and teachers while Erica and I filled out enrollment forms and learned where her homeroom would be. The principal and Scott escorted her there, and that was the beginning of the rest of her high school career.

On our next stop of the day Marvin introduced me to Bill, his accountant, told him I used to be a bookkeeper, and said he thought I'd do a good job. Then Bill and I talked shop. That's when I found out about the March 15th tax deadline for farmers and that they reported on a cash rather than an accrual basis. *Oh, thank goodness. That'll be a lot easier.* In cash accounting, expenses such as wheat seed are recognized when they're paid, and the income is recognized when it's received.

"Well," Bill said, "this'll be great. Most of the farmers just bring in shoe boxes full of receipts and grain contracts. We have to sort them out. But if you do that part and bring in a yearly farm income and expense statement, as well as your personal deductions, we won't have to bill you so much."

You're darn tootin' I thought. *It'll save you hours and hours of work.*

When we left there, we went to The Hearty Rancher for lunch, and I brought up the need for specialized journal and ledger forms and binders.

"Why can't you just use yellow legal pads?" Marvin asked.

"I can't. Even if I turn them sideways, they don't have the lines I'll need for columns for income and different sorts of expenses to match up to the income tax forms. And they won't be sturdy enough."

"Oh," he said. So we went to the office supply store in nearby (31 miles away) Fort Morgan, got the supplies, and stopped for ice cream at the Dairy Queen before heading home.

I figured out a chart of accounts that would keep the business income and expenses separate from the personal ones. And it would be accurate. When I asked Marvin where he kept the cancelled checks, receipts, and papers about wheat sales, he showed me a box full of papers and envelopes.

Just like Bill had said.

I should have known.

Part of a farm wife's job.

A Nice Quiet Lunch

TWO DAYS LATER I called Virginia, my new sister-in-law, and invited her and her husband Eldred to lunch. On the appointed day they arrived with Bear, their toy poodle.

Over lunch we chatted about the farm and other farmers.

"Looks like the wheat's coming up pretty good," Eldred commented.

"Yeah," Marvin said, "except for one of the fields south of the house. It's a little slower than the rest, but I think it'll come along."

As a brand new farm wife, I didn't have anything to add to the conversation.

Virginia chimed in. "We went by Rick's place on the way down here. Some of his fields are slow, too."

"Well, if the weather…" He was interrupted by a huge racket in the back part of the house. We all ran to see what was going on. By the time we got there, all we could see was a big ball of fur, tumbling off Erica's bed and out of her room, with barking, yipping, whining, spitting, hissing. Curly orange cat fur and gray and white dog fur was flying everywhere. When the ball finally rolled to a stop all the way across the adjoining room, the two combatants split apart and ran their own ways—Bear to Virginia and Puddy Tat to a dark corner of Erica's closet.

As calm returned we went back to our lunch. But this time there was no talk of farming.

"Wow," said Marvin. "That looked just like the cat and dog fights you see in movie cartoons."

"Virginia?" I asked. "Is Bear okay? Did he get any scratches or bites?"

"No." She looked at the shivering bundle in her lap. "He'll be fine once he calms down."

"How about the cat?" Eldred asked.

"Well," I replied, "I think she's probably okay, but I'm not going to check on her until she's had a chance to settle down. She must have been asleep on the bed, and when Bear jumped up to investigate this new scent, he woke her up. I'm just glad there won't be vet bills for either one."

After that, whenever Bear came to visit, he'd walk cautiously through every door and around every corner. No more impulsive jumps.

I was glad the incident hadn't happened during our wedding.

Going Over the Ground – April 1982

THE MONTH AFTER our wedding Marvin announced that he'd be going to the section the next day to go over the part that had lain fallow last year. "Bring me lunch around noon," he said.

"Okay," I said, "but how will I find you?"

"Look for the tractor. I don't think anyone else will be working ground this early. Just go up the Baseline Road until you see me."

The next day it seemed simple enough. Although Marvin had more than 3,000 acres, the section was fairly close to the house. I knew where the Baseline Road was and that the tractor was big and red. I made a couple of sandwiches, put in a fruit cup, added some chips and a couple of cookies. Off I went in the pickup, turning north out of the yard, then west onto the Baseline. It wasn't long until I saw a red tractor, but it looked like I needed to turn north onto another road so I could intercept it. I couldn't see any other red tractor, so I made that turn to the north and parked by the side of the road waiting as the tractor approached.

The closer it got, the more uncertain I became. Something didn't feel right. Finally, it was close enough that I could see it was the wrong man driving it! What to do now?

I hightailed it back to the Baseline and headed west again alternately speeding up because I didn't want to be late with Marvin's lunch and then slowing down because I didn't want to miss his red tractor. People who don't live on the prairie think the land is completely flat, but it's furrowed with downs and ups, dip and rises, short hills and miniature valleys. I could miss him easily if he was in one of the downs, dips, or valleys.

Finally, just showing above a small rise I spotted the tractor—a Massey 4800—heading for the Baseline. Soon, I was certain I'd found the right one.

"You have to get the pickup off the road," he yelled out the tractor door and pointed. "There's a drive over that way. Pull into it just enough so you aren't on the road anymore. I'll come down and pick you up."

"Pick me up?" I had no idea what was about to happen.

I drove slowly *over that way*, looking for a driveway across the barrow ditch beside the road. The only way I finally found it was by spotting the tracks the tractor tires had made through the weeds when Marvin pulled off the road and into the field. I parked the pickup, left the keys in it—I'd already learned that keys were to be left in ignitions in all vehicles at the farm—and walked across to the tractor. Marvin was already in the small jump seat behind and to the right of the driver's seat. "Hand me my lunch and"—he pointed to the seat he'd just vacated—"get in."

"Why?"

"You have to learn to drive it."

Oh shit.

"Don't worry. Twelve-year-old kids learn how to do this."

He ate his lunch and told me what all the levers were for. There were gears. Throttle.

Hydraulics that lowered and lifted the 24-foot-wide implement in and out of the ground, and another set that folded the implement so it could be towed down the road.

Then it was time for the real stuff. We changed places. He put it in gear, pushed the throttle forward and lowered the chisels into the ground. And away we went! At about five and a half miles per hour. Turning under old wheat stubble and opening the soil for what was to be the first of many such days, I watched how he managed the turns at the edges of the field. I listened carefully to the sounds the big diesel engine made as he maneuvered the monster tractor through the turns. Throttle down and lift implement, turn, straighten, throttle up and lower implement. Like dance steps. Listen to the music.

I learned that the shanks on the implement were one foot apart but the two rows of them were offset by six inches. The shanks could hold chisels or sweeps or the discs that would be used later in the year to cut up large amounts of straw. First, we chiseled the fields. Later we would replace the chisels with the 18-inch sweeps, and work over the ground several more times until it was ready for planting in September.

As we went back and forth across the 360 acres, I told him about my encounter with the other farmer. He laughed. "Shoemaker, probably. We'll see what he has to say next time we're in town for lunch."

Eventually, we traded seats again and I ran the tractor while Marvin coached from the jump seat.

I finally gained enough skill so I could work a field all day—even doing the turns gracefully. The only time I ever had trouble was when I saw Marvin sitting in the pickup, waiting to trade with me. Then my coordination went to jelly. The first few times I stopped the tractor before I even reached the edge of the field so he wouldn't see me blow the turn.

Then I worked up enough nerve to do the turn while he was watching. Naturally, I screwed it up, very nearly took out part of the road, and had to stop with the implement in the ground. *Bad farm wife! Bad!* The only thing he said was, "Wellwhudjadothatfor?"

I kept practicing, though, and one day I did the turn perfectly—right in front of my farmer! *Proud farm wife! Proud!* No more performance anxiety.

It was a glorious thing to do—making those marks in the earth in preparation for planting another crop of wheat to feed people all over the world.

Going to Town – April 1982

GOING TO TOWN was a weekly event. For the first couple of weeks of our marriage, Marvin went with me. One time we found that rain the previous night had turned the three ruts of the gravel road into slippery mush. "Hmmm," Marvin said as the pickup slithered along the road. "A little slick."

With his window down, he was looking at the rows of wheat growing in our fields. I was petrified, staring out the windshield with one hand bracing myself on the dashboard and the other holding a death grip on the elbow rest of the door. I was sure we were about to be horribly maimed or dead.

By the next Monday when we went to town, the mud had turned to dust. Marvin showed me the hospital and the doctor's office, the fire station, gas station, grocery store, post office, drug store, parts store, clothing store, Methodist church, VFW, and the grain elevator.

The grain elevator was easy. Like all small prairie settlements, the grain elevator was the tallest thing in town. In Akron it anchored the south end of Main Street. Most of the other places were clustered along the highway and Main Street.

Marvin made a point to give me special instructions about the volunteer fire station. "If you hear the fire whistle go off, get off the road. The firemen will be coming to the station fast—really fast. They come from all directions, and when they get here, they jump out of their vehicles, leaving them wherever—sometimes in the middle of a street."

"Isn't that dangerous?"

"Only if you get in front of them. After the fire trucks leave, other people park the firemen's cars out of the way."

He stopped at the gas station and introduced me and my red Jeep Wagoneer to the owner. Then we repeated the process at the parts store. I didn't know why Marvin was making such a point of introducing me around like that.

The first time I went to town by myself I found out. I pulled into the gas station. The attendant came out, filled the tank, looked under the hood, washed the windows, and then came to the driver's side and knocked on the top of the car. I held out money for the gas.

"Don't need that," he said. "I'll write it down to Marvin. You're good to go."

"Oh."

My next stop was the parts store. I handed the list to the man behind the counter who promptly disappeared into the rows of shelves. No such thing as self-service here either. He brought the parts, helped me load them in the car, and said, "I'll write it down to Marvin."

Oh. That proved Marvin had good credit. I made a vow to promptly pay the monthly invoices from the places we had accounts.

I quickly became familiar with the other businesses. It was nice being greeted by name by clerks and other shoppers, and I looked forward to my weekly trips. I learned to keep a well-stocked pantry and freezer because, if I forgot to get something, we did without it for the week.

Honey, Come Quick! – April 1982

THE DAY AFTER our wedding, Marvin had sternly insisted that I always wear my shoes in the house—no running around barefoot. "If I holler for you to come quick, I mean it, and you can't waste time getting your shoes on."

"B-b-b-but," I stuttered, "why?"

"You never know when something might happen, and I need help in a hurry. Remember, we're a long way from town and neighbors. There might be a grass or wheat fire or an engine fire. A fence might be down. The cows might get out. Lightning, tornados, hail. We never know."

"Oh." I considered all the potential perils I was in for. "Okay." I sure didn't want to get my feet full of burrs or goat-heads. Those invasive goat-heads were also called *puncture vines*—for a very good reason: they're sturdy enough to burst a bicycle tire. And I didn't want to fight a fire bare-footed anyway.

So, one day I heard the pickup come boiling into the yard, roaring around the house, and sliding to a stop beside the kitchen door. "Honey, come quick!" I turned off the oven where cookies were baking and ran to the pickup. Away we went!

Was it a fire? Were the cows out?

A little way down the road, he slowed and pointed at the fence line. "Look," he said and turned off the engine. I was expecting a dire emergency, but there I saw a mother racoon with her four little bandits staring at us from the tall grass around a fence post.

How wonderful that my man took the time to show me this beautiful scene!

When we got back to the house, the cookies were ruined, but it was a small price to pay for the joy of that moment.

A Farm Auction and a Donkey – April 1982

WE HADN'T BEEN married more than a couple of weeks when Marvin and I went to a farm auction. I didn't know anyone there, but most of them seemed to know me. As everyone gathered before the business at hand, the women greeted me, and many welcomed me to the

Methodist Church. I wasn't sure why they thought I was or should be a Methodist until Marvin let me know that all the Alishouses in Akron had always been Methodists.

Hmmm. Did any of them even wonder if I might be Jewish or Catholic or Mormon or Hindu or atheist?

"Hey Marvin," several of the men said, "this must be your new hired hand."

At least I now knew what that question they'd all been asking well before the wedding was all about. We had a good laugh over it.

I'd gone to many indoor auctions when I lived in Boulder and then in Denver. There I found lots of treasures: hand-crafted things, artworks, antiques, Persian rugs, and a lot of miscellaneous "stuff." I learned not to wave my hand in the air unless I wanted to bid on something.

Here, in the country, the auctioneer pattered his way through household goods and furniture. I noticed that most of the men did the bidding, but their womenfolk would give them nudges now and then.

Next we moved on to auctioning off nuts and bolts, shop equipment, machine parts, tires, pickups, and farm machinery. And a donkey.

"Oh, he's soooo cute! Marvin, can we buy the donkey?"

"We don't need a donkey."

But then the people around us started in on him: "Come on, Marvin, let her have the donkey." "Don't be a cheapskate—buy her the donkey."

Finally he shut everybody up by looking straight at me and saying, "Fine. We'll buy it, but you're the one who's going to have to take care of it."

That settled it. I had no idea what to do with a donkey, so that was the end of that.

Land

THE PEOPLE WHO'D lived on this farm were getting on in years and were moving to town. None of their children wanted to farm the place, so the land was also for sale.

I thought about land.

In the early 1900s Marvin's paternal grandparents rented a railroad boxcar for their belongings and moved from Missouri to eastern Colorado. I'd seen a photo of the shack they built on their forty-acre homestead parcel. The scene showed bare dirt. Through an open front door you could see the back wall of the house with about a four-inch gap between the wall and the dirt floor—more than wide enough for rattlesnakes to slide in without a problem.

And the one-room house was small. As Marvin said, "You could throw a cat across it." There were no trees on this prairie, so I had no idea where they'd gotten the wood to build it.

How unprepared they were, with no idea about the high-plains climate that could produce fierce lightning, deadly tornados, and torrential rains interspersed with dry winds that sucked the moisture out of the soil. Did they try to use the same farming methods that had worked in Missouri where they had twenty-two inches of rain a year and lots of humus in the soil? Here they'd be lucky to get half that much rain. Native prairie plants sent their roots deep down in order to survive.

Marvin knew from family lore that they'd dug a well by hand. They had to go down twenty feet before they hit water. How, I wondered, did they know where to dig?

With their single-bottom horse-drawn plow they broke out a one-acre plot for a garden and two ten-acre fields: one for wheat and one for corn—their cash crops. In order to break the sod, they had to go over the fields multiple times. The rest of their land was left for pasture. At least the short grass of the prairie pasture was nutritious for the livestock. But they had no stock of hay built up to feed their horses and cows during the winter blizzards.

How did they keep warm? Did they bring enough canned goods to see them through until they could grow a garden? To take a wagon to town to get supplies was an overnight trip. They were about seventeen miles from town as the crow flies, and there were no roads.

These pioneers came here only three generations ago and built farms and lives with manpower, womanpower, horsepower, and clumsy machinery. They relied on themselves and their neighbors as they built houses, schools, and churches—a community. In spite of all the hardships, they were able to prove up on their homestead quarter and later buy more land—the land we now farmed.

When we got back to our farm, our land, later that day, I looked around and saw it with new eyes. Even without a donkey, it was a great place.

Putting in a Garden – April 1982

ONE DAY, MARVIN asked if I wanted to grow a garden. I'd been so busy I hadn't even thought about it until then.

"Yes," I said. "Is there any special place you'd like me to put it?"

He motioned out toward the south of the house. "How about right there? That's where we've done it before."

The weedy patch next to the old cinder-block chicken house didn't look like it had ever been a garden. "I'll go dig up the soil," he said as he headed out toward the big shop building. I figured he had a rototiller there, so I went to inspect my future garden.

The chicken house would be a good place to keep my tools and supplies. It even had a couple of windows on the south side, where I could put seedlings to harden off, and there was a spigot for a hose. Everything I needed.

As I stepped back outside, Marvin came around the chicken house in the tractor with the chisels.

Oh, no! How big is this garden going to be?

He backed up—implement even with the back side of the chicken house—lowered the twenty-four feet of chisels into the ground and moved forward about sixteen feet. "Is that big enough," he yelled over the roar of the tractor. I nodded, thinking it was time for me to find a shovel and start busting up the big clods, But Marvin motioned me out of the way. He folded up one section of the implement, which left only sixteen feet of chisels and maneuvered the tractor so he could go over the plot again at a ninety-degree angle to the first pass. And there it was—a roughed in garden plot!

It turned out that he did have a rototiller, and it was a lot easier to use after the initial passes with the chisels. Soon the sandy loam was ready. I planted tomatoes, potatoes, carrots, parsnips, cabbage, radishes, lettuces, onions, peas, beans, and herbs. Somehow, the garden didn't look right, so I found some chicken wire and old wooden posts to build a rustic little fence along the north side and planted sweet peas to grow on it. Then there was a little room on the south side, so I planted Sweet Williams and a bunch of iris.

Some neighbors and some family members expressed clear opinions about flowers not belonging in vegetable gardens, but I kept the flowers anyway. And it was always a beautiful, bountiful garden.

Not Farm Wife Material – Revisited

THE CABINETS IN one corner of the bathroom went from floor to ceiling and consisted of four big cubes. They were great for towels and sheets, but there were no smaller shelves where I could organize things like toothpaste, shampoo, medicines, band aids, and so on. I asked Marvin if he minded my remodeling them. He said it was fine with him, although I could tell he wondered why it was necessary, and I set to work drawing my plans and making a list of materials.

The next time we went to town for groceries, I picked up a sheet of plywood and some paint. We already had the other stuff I needed. At home, I put away the groceries and started supper in the crockpot. Then I got to work.

I brought out the circular saw and a long extension cord, wrestled the plywood onto the top of the redwood picnic table by the kitchen door, measured, snapped a chalk line for my first cut. Marvin was working on something in the shop, so I didn't bother him for help. Didn't need help anyway.

I moved the plywood so the saw wouldn't cut into the table and found some bricks to stack on the benches to support the part I was sawing off. Then I climbed on top of the plywood so I could use my weight to hold the sheet steady. I began the cut with my circular saw. About half-way through, Mommy (my mother-in-law, the one who had told Marvin before we were married she didn't think I was farm material) drove into the yard. I stopped cutting. Our eyes met as she stopped her car. At that moment I knew she had changed her mind.

She was a wonderful mother-in-law, and I tried my best to be a good daughter-in-law.

Here Come the Cows

EARLY IN APRIL, Marvin and I rode through the pastures to see if the grass was growing well enough to support cows. His land could support 120 cow-calf pairs, more or less, depending on how healthy the grass was, which depended on the weather. After we bumped around for a while, he pronounced the grass to be in good condition.

The fences, however, were not. There were three places that needed to be fixed.

Uh-oh, I thought. *Is this going to be my next lesson?*

"I'll need a few new fence posts. Probably metal ones. They cost more, but last longer, and it's easier to tie barbed wire to them. The cedar ones are durable, but it's hard to hammer staples into them. I've hit my thumb plenty of times trying to do it."

"Yep." *I was right. This was going to be my next lesson. At least I won't be banging my thumb.*

Then we went to check on the windmill that pumped water into the big tank for the cows. Marvin fiddled with some connection, found some problems, and announced that he'd have to call Lloyd, the man who kept most of the windmills in the area working.

"Where will the cows come from?" I asked as we headed back to the house.

"David," he said, tilting his head toward the northeast. "He's one of our neighbors over that way. He rents the pasture. Doesn't have a lot of cows, so he brings them here in his stock trailer and makes several trips. Doesn't need a semi, and it's easier on the cows."

More information for me to digest.

When we got back to the house, Marvin made a couple of phone calls—this was long before the advent of cell phones—setting up dates for windmill repairs as soon as possible and cows toward the end of the month, and then we went to town to get fence posts and a good pair of leather gloves for me. On the way back we stopped at the "corner," which was a half-mile north of the house at the Baseline Road. There was an old scruffy windbreak of elm trees, most of them dying, an old cinderblock barn that was once used for pigs, and the rubble-filled cellar of a house that had been moved. Marvin kept a stock of barbed wire close to the barn. We loaded some rolls of it into the pickup. I was glad I had the new gloves.

~ ~ ~

BARBED WIRE. SCARY stuff. It always reminded me of the day my grandpa in Mississippi put a halter and rope on a young calf and told me to let her eat the tall grass along outside the pasture fence. I was about ten years old. Why Grandpa thought I could control a calf that weighed considerably more than I did, I'll never know.

"And don't let go of the rope," he admonished.

That calf didn't want to eat the nice green grass. She only wanted to get back into the pasture and go to her mother. She dragged me along next to the fence as she searched for a hole to get through. Finally she found a place where the lower strand of barbed wire sagged down a bit. She stuck her head through that hole and struggled through the fence.

I held on to the rope as long as I could, but finally let go when my palms got bloody from a bad rope burn. I was a mess. Grandpa wasn't happy with me. He thought I should have been tougher than that.

~ ~ ~

BY THE TIME Marvin and I got home, it was getting late. The kids were home from school, so it was time for me to start thinking about making supper and supervising homework.

"We'll get an early start on the fences tomorrow," Marvin said. "There aren't too many places we need to work on, so it won't take too long."

Oh shit, I thought. *Will I live through this?*

The next morning, first thing, we pulled the old posts out and put in new ones. That seemed easy enough, but then things got scary, and I again pondered my life expectancy.

Marvin slipped a roll of barbed wire onto a steel rod in the bed of the pickup and anchored the rod into some holders along the sides of the pickup bed. At the first new post he stopped next to the fence and wrapped the end of the wire around the post. Then he said, "I'm going to drive across this draw to where that cedar post is leaning over. You get in the back of the pickup and keep the wire from getting tangled as it unrolls onto the ground." He handed me a shorted steel bar. "You can use this to keep the roll from sliding from side to side on the rod."

"Um, how fast are you going to go?"

"Not very."

"Will you slow down if I yell?"

"Sure.

He got in the driver's seat and started slowly toward the leaning cedar post. As the pickup swayed from side to side, the wire roll kept sliding back and forth, and I kept trying to keep it toward the side of the pickup that was closest to the fence line.

"Slow down!"

"Why?"

"It's tangled."

He stopped. We untangled the wire. He got in the back of the pickup with the steel rod and told me to drive. With the ease of many years of practice, he kept the roll where it was supposed to be. We arrived at the cedar post. I was not maimed. Whew!

We fastened the barbed wire with wire ties to the posts about a foot off the ground. Then we repeated the process two more times until we had a three-wire fence, and after that we had only two more sections to fix. I decided fixing fence was not nearly as enjoyable as driving the tractor.

On the way home Marvin told me, "It's hard to get the tension on the wires right when the fence runs through a draw. If it's too tight, it's hard to pull down to attach to the posts at the right height. If it's too loose, it sags." Farm wisdom.

A couple of days later I was home alone when I heard a truck coming into the drive. He stopped politely by the front door until I came out to meet him. There was a windmill logo on his pickup. He introduced himself and said, unnecessarily, that he had come to fix the windmill. I began telling him how to get to it. "Go through the gate over there and follow the fence to the next gate, then turn right and …" He was staring at me. "Oh, duh," I said. "You know how to get there better than I do, don't you?"

He grinned. "Yep."

He went to the windmill, and I went back into the house.

Finally the day arrived for David to bring his cows to our pasture. It was anti-climactic. Each time David brought a load, he drove into the pasture and opened the end gate of his trailer. The cows walked out and bawled until mamas and calves found each other. Then they walked away and started grazing.

It was good to know they'd be safe behind that newly repaired fence.

Dancing at the VFW – May 1982

THE THING TO do on Saturday night, at least for those folks who wanted a "rip-roarin" good time, was to go to the dance at the VFW lounge. The music was mostly country-western with some rock and roll tucked in here and there. The bands were all from northeastern Colorado. The dancers were in their forties, fifties, sixties, seventies—and even a few in their eighties. The crowd was quite diverse. It included farmers, bankers, contractors, shopkeepers, teachers, and so on. The room was dimly lit, loud, smoky, and hot. I found out later one of the waitresses was also the nurse at the doctor's office. She was good at giving shots—medicine or liquor.

At first, most of the men seemed to feel they needed to ask me to dance—sort of a welcome to the rowdy bunch. Quite a welcome! Some of them just wanted to feel me up and find out how far they were likely to get. Not that I was anything special, just new. Most were friendly and very strong, even the old ones. They squeezed me and whirled me, and one even picked me up and threw me back to Marvin. I guess he didn't like the way I danced.

Marvin and I were both in good physical condition and could do a lot of the fancy dance moves. The one we liked best was the "pretzel." Of course, everyone got on the dance floor for the Chicken Dance and the conga lines. Slow dances, known as buckle polishers, invariably involved a few "dips."

We got a little drunk, sometimes more than a little, but that much physical activity burned up the alcohol in a hurry.

When the band stopped playing at one a.m., we went to The Hearty Rancher for breakfast, then headed home, driving south and watching the meteor showers—especially the Perseides during August. Once we got to the Baseline Road there was no more traffic, so sometimes we pulled off the deserted road and stopped and …

An Insert from Erica – Early June 1982

In 1982 my mom married a farmer, which meant I had a new dad. Up until that point I had never had a little brother and I had only the vaguest notion of what to do with one. When Dad told us one hot day that first summer to go up to the windmill and clean out the stock tank—"It's full of seaweed," he said—we collected a shovel and a couple of rakes and jumped in the pickup. I seized the opportunity to drive because that's what you do when you're 14 years old. Scott was good natured and didn't complain.

We drove through the pasture over hillocks, cow trails, and cow pies to get to the windmill. A shovel and a couple rakes to clean out the seaweed and other gunk. Prior to then I didn't know that seaweed will actually grow in freshwater in a stock tank. Of course I know now it wasn't saltwater seaweed, but that green algae stuff sure did look like it belonged in the ocean. We got busy raking and shoveling the green goop out and dropping it on the ground around the tank. The cows weren't going to eat it, so it would just rot where it was.

Eventually we sat down for a little bit to rest on the edge of the concrete slab. It had rained the day before and there were puddles in the dirt from the hooves of cows coming to drink. Puddles where we'd dumped the green goop. We were quiet, each of us thinking our own thoughts. It took a few minutes, but I finally noticed that the puddle in front of us was moving. Was I imagining things? "Scott, take a look at that puddle and tell me if there's something alive in there."

"Yeah, something's moving." He pointed to the next puddle. "And that one over there, and another one over there."

"Go stick your hand in," I ordered, "and find out what it is."

"I'm not sticking my hand in there!"

So we got one of the shovels to scoop out the mud. It turned out that there were a bunch of tadpoles wriggling about. They were big, about the size of the end of my thumb. The puddles were drying up in the hot sun and we couldn't allow them to die.

I sent Scott back to the farm to get some sort of container so we could take them back to the small tank near the house which always had running water. While he was gone, I splashed water on the tadpoles to keep them safe. He came back with a great big glass jar that had a lid on it, so we scooped up as many tadpoles as we possibly could out of all the different puddles.

That jar turned out to be the one that mom made sun tea in. By the time we finished, it had dents in the lid from us trying—unsuccessfully—to poke air holes. I finally told her years later that Scott and I were the ones who'd dented the lid. "I figured as much," was all she said.

A couple days later, we went out to the stock tank in the corral to check on our little guys, but they were all gone. We were sad, but nature takes its course. It was just one of those lessons learned early by people who live on farms.

After a few weeks it rained and anyone who knows a farmer knows they always go outside to check how much moisture we'd received. Scott and I stepped outside with Dad that morning. We could hear frogs singing, just chirping away, happy as frogs will always be in the rain.

Dad said, "Where'd all those damn frogs come from?" Scott and I just grinned at each other behind him and kept quiet.

I Become a Truck Driver – June 1982

"**YOU NEED TO** be able to drive the grain trucks back and forth between the wheat fields and the bins at the house," Marvin announced as we rolled out of bed one morning.

Here we go again. But it can't be as scary as barbed wire.

When breakfast was finished we went to the shop, and school began with me and the red two-ton Ford truck that held 400 bushels of wheat and had a four-speed over-and-under transmission.

"How old is it?" I asked.

Marvin thought for a bit. "I'm not sure. Maybe 1960 or 1961."

"That's about when I graduated from high school, but if it's gotten good maintenance, it can last even longer." Later I developed a sort of love/hate relationship with this red Ford.

It took me a while to figure out the gear shift. The shifting pattern was like a capital H. When in neutral, the shifting lever flopped back and forth across the horizontal crosspiece of the H. *So far, so good. This was just like the 1957 Chevy I learned to drive on.* But then came the big difference. Attached to the gearshift was a switch to change the transmission level from Lo to Hi. If that switch was in Lo, the top left point of the H was LoFirst (sometimes referred to as Granny or LoLo), which was for getting the truck moving with a heavy load in soft dirt. From there the gears went to LoSecond at the bottom left point of the H, then to LoThird on the upper right, and LoFourth on the bottom right.

At that point I had to flip the switch to Hi range and repeat the pattern for HiFifth through HiEighth—eight gears in all.

The truck wasn't loaded, but in order to get the feel of it, I started in LoFirst. The gearshift was about six inches to the right of the big steering wheel. I pulled the handle down into LoSecond, and the shifter was about eight inches to the right of my thigh. Then I pushed the gearshift up and over the H to the right. In LoThird the truck began picking up speed, but those last two gears positioned the long shifting lever about two feet to the right of my body, which meant I couldn't use my body weight as leverage to get the gearshift INTO those gears.

What was I going to do? I knew I had to figure out a way to shift the gears without ruining my right arm and shoulder.

The first thing I had to take care of, though, was the cracked plastic seat cover that pinched my bottom every time I changed position. I found a sturdy (and dirty) old couch cushion that fit the seat perfectly, saving me considerable wear and tear. I found that I could wiggle over to the far right side of the cushion to change the gears that were hard to reach—and I could still hold onto the steering wheel and reach the clutch with my left foot.

One other thing needed to be fixed. The steering wheel cover had a crack in it. The inner steel core was intact, but that doggone crack caught my finger every time I slid my hand across it, so I patched it with electrical tape. It looked sort of hit-or-miss, but I didn't care. *Now I won't lose a finger.* All set.

I used up a lot of gas driving up and down the road and around the yard going forward and backward and practicing turning corners.

Marvin showed me how to back up the grain auger properly so that the small gate at the back of the truck was centered on the hopper and the wheat would pour into the hopper that held the auger that lifted the wheat to the hole in the top of the storage bin. Of course, Marvin had been practicing this since he was a boy.

I couldn't for the life of me get the truck lined up properly. There was no way I could see the hopper in the side mirrors because it was a lot narrower than the truck.

Not to worry. Resourceful Farm Wife asked Marvin to put the truck into position. Then she found some boards to place on the ground beside the tires. Aha! Problem solved. I could use the boards as a guide and back in easily and accurately.

Then I had to learn to turn on the small tractor that powered the P.T.O. (power take-off) that turned the augur that carried the wheat to the top of the bin. Marvin warned me not to wear loose clothing and not to get too close to the P.T.O. "Clothes and fingers can get caught. People who are careless around a P.T.O. lose their arms. When the truck is backed up, start the P.T.O., then open the back gate of the truck. Once the flow gets started and takes some weight off the back end, pull the lever on the floor at the left of the driver's seat to engage the hydraulic lift to raise the bed of the truck in increments as the truck empties."

Whew! Clear as mud, I thought, but I practiced as much as I could without any wheat in the truck, and by harvest time I knew fairly well what to do and when to do it.

After all that work, it turned out I didn't drive the truck very much until several years later. Scott was fully capable of driving our truck back and forth between the field and the auger, and, of course, the harvest crew knew the routine. I ran the P.T.O., stood beside the hopper, directed them to right or left, and signaled when to stop and when to lift the truck bed. Most of the drivers for the harvest crew only sat in their cabs and raised their truck bed when I signaled, but when Scott brought in a load, he'd get out and talk to me. I think he felt sorry for me the first couple of years. After that we just enjoyed our conversations.

Learning to Run the Combine

MARVIN HAD BEEN checking the combine and making small repairs so it wouldn't need a large overhaul during harvest. I was busy in the house until he showed up at the kitchen door.

"Honey, come quick. I need some help with the combine."

As we walked to the shop, he explained the help he needed—nothing serious, thank goodness. He only needed me to hold one pair of pliers tight on a piece of metal while he used another pair of pliers to turn a bolt until it loosened. Easy.

"Is that all?" I asked. I was ready to turn around and go back to the house.

"Well, no. I've been thinking you should learn to operate the combine."

Here we go again. I had learned how to operate the tractor with chisels, sweeps, anhydrous applicator tubes, and drills; then the trucks and augers; now the combine. And here came the problem. The combine had way more moving parts than any of the other machines.

"First," he said, "I need to tell you how hydraulics work."

"You didn't tell me about them when I was learning to use the tractor."

"All you needed to know then was how to get the implement in the ground and out of the ground, and you did a good job."

Good Farm Wife.

"You'll be able to work these just fine, too. Climb up in the cab."

I climbed the steps up to the small platform on the left side of the combine, opened the door, and took my place on the seat. Marvin followed and stood in the doorway, hunched over, showing me the various controls.

"That big handle over there on the right turns on the machine—all the separate parts that harvest the wheat. When you start it, be sure it's in idle. Once everything's running, you're ready to cut."

"Got it."

"That wide thing on the front of the combine is the header. It goes up and down by moving this handle back and forth. Got that?"

"I think so."

I figured out why the machine was called a combine. It combined several machines into one. I thought that was all there was to it. Big mistake.

There was a lot more involved, as I would eventually learn.

"How do I make the whole thing move?"

"Don't get in so much of a hurry. You're nowhere near ready to move it yet. Climb down and I'll show you what each part of the machine does."

I followed him to the front of the beast. He started pointing.

"The header includes the reel that rotates to pull the wheat stalks onto the header platform so the sickle blade can cut them off. Behind the reel is the platform auger"—point—"that moves all the cut wheat into the throat. That's the big part right behind the center of the platform auger at the back of the header. There's a feeder chain inside the throat that moves the stalks and heads into the cylinder."

"Where's the cylinder?"

"Inside the body of the combine. It's hard to see from here."

So he led me to the back of the combine and pointed at the cylinder.

"What does it do?"

"It separates the wheat kernels from the chaff. Then everything moves across the sieves. Those are the big metal plates with holes in them that move back and forth. There's a fan below them that blows the chaff up and out the back of the combine onto the ground. The kernels fall through the sieves down into another auger which lifts them into the grain bin"—he pointed yet again—"on the top of the combine."

I wasn't quite overwhelmed yet, but almost.

"Mostly all of this is automatic. All you have to do is control the ground speed, combine speed, header height, and reel height."

Of course. Clear as mud—one of my grandmother's favorite sayings.

"Okay," I said.

We went back to the cab.

"Now, about the hydraulics. When you push the lever forward, it'll keep pumping hydraulic fluid into the cylinder until you release the handle. If you keep the lever forward, the header will go lower and lower until it digs into the ground and gobbles up a bunch of dirt—which you will then have to clean out of the whole combine."

"Oh shit."

"Yeah. It takes a lot of time and hard work, so don't let it happen."

I silently vowed to pay close attention to the header at all times. I didn't want to hear Marvin say, "Wellwhudjadothatfor?"

That evening while Marvin and Scott were watching TV, I was busy with a pad of yellow paper making a schematic drawing that I thought was like all the parts Marvin had told me about. Drawing always helps me remember.

~ ~ ~

THE NEXT MORNING Marvin showed me how to start the engine and put the combine into reverse. I backed it slowly out of the shop, then put it into forward gear and drove around the yard while I practiced using the Hydrostatic Drive to increase or decrease speed without changing gears. After a while he went down the steps and onto the ground. I practiced some more, then drove up beside him and stopped.

"Now can I learn how to work the header?"

"Okay." He climbed up beside me. "Grab that big lever and push it down."

I did and nearly jumped out of my skin. "Holy cow! It sure is noisy."

"Yeah, and it'll get louder when it's revved up and working."

He was right. I moved the throttle up a little, then a little more, stopping when Marvin told me to. "Listen to the sound and look where the throttle is, so you'll know where it should be when you're cutting wheat."

Got it.

"Now it's time for you to move the header up and down." He pointed. "Use that lever."

This was the scary part for me. I pulled back gingerly on the lever. Nothing happened at first, but then the header started rising. And kept rising. And kept on rising.

"Oops," I said and let go of the lever.

The header stopped.

"It's okay," Marvin assured me. "Just push the lever forward until the header is about a foot off the ground, then let go."

I was so nervous I pushed it only a little way forward, then another tiny bit. It didn't move very much, so I pushed it farther, and the header started going down faster. Too fast. I let go.

"I'm afraid it's going to dig into the dirt."

"No, you're doing just fine. Try again. You just need to practice. And, besides, the combine isn't moving, so the header won't be able to pick up any dirt. It'll just try to keep going down."

"Okay," I said as he moved away toward the shop.

I practiced and practiced moving the header. Then I practiced and practiced moving the reel. Then I played with the levers until I could put the header and reel exactly where I wanted them.

"Ha," I said with a big grin as Marvin appeared at the shop doors.

"Okay," he called. "Now put it in gear and work the levers while you're moving."

I practiced more, getting used to the rhythms of movement and sound that told me what the machine was doing. Lovely. Now I knew what to do, but not when to do it.

~ ~ ~

MY NEXT LESSON wouldn't come until harvest was in full gear. I took Marvin's lunch to him in the field he was cutting. He told me to get in the combine and cut while he stood in the door and ate. And coached me.

"You want the header a little below the heads of wheat, and the reel needs to be where it'll sweep the stalks into the sickle bars."

That made sense, and suddenly I was cutting wheat—adjusting the header and reel to accommodate taller and shorter areas of wheat. If the header was too low it would knock the kernels out of the heads; if too high it would miss the heads and the wheat wouldn't be cut.

"Now we're coming to a gulley up ahead. Let me get in the seat and show you how to get through it. You don't want to miss the wheat on the downhill side or run the header into the dirt on the uphill side." He slowed down, lowered the header, then lifted it. And never missed a head.

We changed positions so I could practice going across the next gulley. I went much slower than he had, because I was afraid of running the header into the ground on the uphill side, so I raised the header too soon and missed some of the wheat.

"Sometimes the gulley is too deep to do this," he continued. "If that happens, you drive alongside it on both sides. It's called cutting out a gulley."

He looked up into the grain bin. "When you finish this round, you can dump the wheat. That handle on the floor to your left operates the dumping auger."

I slowed as I steered across the cut stubble and approached the truck, moving the auger out so it was at a ninety-degree angle from the combine.

"You're going to move up to the truck bed and position the end of the auger over it where the back wheels are. Then stop." I did.

"Now twist the handle to start the auger." As soon as I did, I got to watch the beautiful stream of grain pouring into the truck.

"Okay. You don't want all the wheat to pour into just one part of the truck, so move the combine forward and back to redistribute the load."

Soon the auger emptied the last of it. I moved it back into position parallel with the combine and was ready to go again.

I didn't get to run the combine very often, but when I did, I enjoyed watching the swaying motion of the standing wheat being pulled in by the reel and listening to the loud rumble of the unloading auger when I dumped my load into a truck. I ran the header into the ground once, but I stopped quickly before the dirt got into the throat, cleared the header, and started cutting again. Whew! Nobody saw me.

Good Farm Wife.

Jobs at Harvest Time – July 1982

HARVEST TIME CAME around every year in early July, and this year was no exception. The wheat planted last September was now ripe and ready to be cut. The past few years had been lean because of drought and grasshoppers and all the other things that can befall a crop before it's safely cut and in the bin. This year's crop was good. We'd gotten just enough rain at the right times to fill the heads of wheat with nice plump kernels. Harvest time was hectic, and everyone had a job to do.

Our harvest crew came from Oklahoma, following the wheat as it ripened from Texas all the way to North Dakota. The same crew had cut wheat for Marvin ever since he began farming. We could see the dust as they came down the Baseline Road. First came a pickup towing a large camping trailer that was home, office, and cook shack. Then came a bright yellow school bus that had been converted into a dorm for the boys of the cutting crew. Last came the grain trucks, each with a combine header in the truck bed and towing a lowboy trailer with a combine on it. Each of these units (truck, header, combine, and trailer) cost about a quarter of a million dollars and was usually driven by a sixteen-year-old boy.

The business was owned by Dale—who bossed the operation, found new business, and paid the bills—and Anna Lou, who cooked for the whole crew. Their son Skip oversaw the cutting operations, bossing the crew of five teenage boys who ran the combines and trucks. The crew also included Skip's two lovely teenage daughters who helped keep the boys in line while working and totally befuddled them when they weren't working. Skip's wife Deborah helped with cooking, going to town for machine parts, and watching over her younger children.

Dale was astonished once when he saw me back the tractor, with its attached implement, perfectly into place. Nobody ever backs such an arrangement perfectly – the trailing object (no matter what it is) always tends to skew to one side or another, which requires the driver to make a kazillion adjustments to the steering wheel. This results in a tango-like dance of the two pieces of machinery. Once I hopped out of the cab, he told me he was going to tell Marvin on me. "*That woman can't back anything,* I'll say. *I had to take over and do it for her.*"

But I knew Marvin wouldn't believe him, so I just laughed along with Dale.

Marvin ran our combine in a separate field. Scott, our youngest son, drove our two grain trucks, hauling the wheat Marvin cut to our storage bins near the house.

I quickly discovered that the only ones keeping records were the custom cutters. They kept track of their truckloads because the total number of bushels were part of the formula that determined their pay.

The bookkeeper in me knew that just wasn't right, so between the truckloads I grabbed a pad of paper from the house and started an on-the-fly system. I kept track of the truckloads, climbing up on each one as it came in to estimate how many bushels it carried. I knew the nominal capacity of each truck, but usually the trucks were overfilled. If a truck was rated at four hundred bushels, it generally carried four-hundred-thirty to four-hundred-fifty bushels. If it was rated at six-hundred-fifty, it probably held seven hundred. The young truck drivers helped me figure this out.

When Scott came in with a truckload, I could tell it was way overloaded because of the sound of the engine. He told me that while he was waiting in the field for his truck to get full, he stomped down the wheat, packing it into the corners of the truck bed. He said it gave him something to do besides swatting flies.

That night I recorded all this information on a paper spreadsheet I devised. There were columns for date, number of bushels, which field the truck came from, whether the truck was one of ours or one from the harvest crew, and which bin it went into. I drew a diagram of the bins and numbered or named them. Occasionally a truck was only partially filled, which happened when it carried the last bit of wheat from a field that was completely cut. I was kept so busy with the record-keeping that after all my practice driving our truck, I didn't have to drive one until a few years later.

The information I recorded was important because it helped determine things like the variety of wheat to plant and how much fertilizer we needed. It also helped us figure out how much wheat we could sell and what our income would be for the year. Marvin always kept back some wheat so we'd have some to sell during a bad harvest year, when the price of wheat generally went higher.

I also had another job. Each year I took a gallon can full of wheat from the first truck. As soon as I had time, and usually because of rain, I washed the wheat and ground it in my hand-cranked mill and baked bread to share with everyone. I figured they deserved to taste some of what they had harvested, so I made it a tradition. After four or five years, Marvin finally told me he didn't like whole wheat bread!

Inside the Combine

ONCE DURING THAT first harvest, I felt that sense of awakening from a dream—a bad dream, in which my pelvic bones were pressing against a metal flange, my legs flailing against nothing. The top part of my body was inside a hot, stinky metal box. Where was I? What had happened? Reality intruded, and I emerged from the dream. There was work to do.

I was on my tummy in the engine compartment of the combine—the combine that cuts the wheat I had watched ripen since March when I'd married Marvin, my farmer husband, the ripe wheat we were now harvesting. Only, the combine had broken down; a hydraulic line had burst. The header, the part that cuts the wheat and pushes it into the cylinders that separate the grain, wouldn't work. Marvin's shoulders were too wide to fit in the compartment, so that job was up to me.

The July heat outside was over eighty degrees. The temp next to the engine was much hotter—the metal was way too hot to touch. We had to fix this monster, so I wiggled farther into the hot, dark, narrow space, relieving the pain on my pelvic bones, and tracing a hydraulic line to find the leak.

I finally saw the place where the line made a ninety-degree turn before it passed through the sheet-metal firewall to the outside where Marvin waited and yelled questions at me. The leak had to be in the corner of the compartment, but I couldn't see it because it was packed full of oil-soaked chaff. Hydraulic oil is the stinkiest stuff there is. *Aha!* I thought. *This'll be a breeze.* Then I found that the packed chaff was *really* packed. I began prying at the solid mass with my fingers, the ones that used to be nicely manicured. Small chunks of chaff came off. Then a big chunk let loose and hit me in the face. My fingers could now trace the line. On the underneath, just before the right-angle bend, I finally felt the split that had brought this mechanical beast to a halt. By this time I was fully awake in the present and wondering how in hell this was happening to me—a woman who used to wear high heels to work at an office in Denver.

Then I was yelling through the firewall telling Marvin where the split was. He disconnected the end of the line on the outside, and we struggled to get his end of the line pushed through the small hole to my side of the firewall.

I scooted backward out of the combine and waited while Marvin made a fast trip to the parts store in town sixteen miles away and a fast trip back with a new line. When he returned, I wiggled back into the bowels of the machine. We wrestled the line through that minuscule hole in the firewall and hooked it up on both ends. Whew!

The combine was ready to cut wheat.

As Marvin pulled out of the yard, I ran to the house, scrubbed some of the chaff and hydraulic oil off my face and hands. Fortunately, nothing had gotten into my eyes. My hair was a mess, but nothing was dripping off it, so I tied a kerchief around my head. Away I ran to my red grain truck to follow Marvin to the field he was cutting. The rhythm of the harvest resumed. I soon had a load of wheat to take to the round-top.

I never worried about manicured nails again.

Mommy and the Lightning Rods – August 1982

ONE SUNDAY WE were at Mommy's house in town along with Marvin's sister and her husband. After downing Mommy's wonderful fried chicken, mashed potatoes, gravy, corn, and pie, the men went to the living room. We women talked as we cleaned up the kitchen.

"We sure are having a lot of thunderstorms this early in the summer." Virginia nodded toward another set of storm clouds building in the east. "This one looks like it could be pretty mean. Probably has some hail in it."

"Hail and lightning," I said. "Marvin said they'd slack off after harvest." I knew harvest wouldn't happen again until early the next July. Hail was always a danger because of the damage it could do to the ripening wheat crop.

"Sometimes they do and sometimes they don't," said Mommy. "When I lived out there, the storms scared me plenty, but John wouldn't spend the money to get lightning rods on the house. One day the lightning rod man came by, and I told him to go ahead and put the rods on."

She nodded to herself. "John didn't notice them for a while, not until the bill came. He fussed about it plenty, but I didn't care. I felt a lot safer."

I'd noticed the rods on the peak of the roof and knew what they were for. But, I'd also noticed that they weren't connected to the ground rods, so they were useless for averting lightning damage. I remembered that Marvin had said he'd put steel siding on his house last summer, so I guessed he hadn't gotten around to getting the ground rods reconnected.

I swear I never called the lightning rod man, but about a week later a man I'd never seen before drove into the yard while I was mowing the lawn. I saw him looking at the unattached ground rods.

He introduced himself. "I come around every year about this time or earlier. Those"—he nodded toward the ground rods—"need to be hooked up. They won't do you any good if they aren't."

"Okay. How much will it cost?"

He named a sum.

"How long will it take?"

"About fifteen minutes. And I'll go up on the roof just to check things there too."

"Okay. Do it. I'll go get the checkbook."

Boy, did I feel powerful, in charge of something like lightning. Wow!

When Marvin came home, I told him what I'd done and why I'd done it.

"How much did it cost?"

I told him.

"Okay. I guess it'll make you feel better."

It did.

At another family gathering I found out a little more about Mommy's story. She said that months after she had the lightning rods installed, John asked her if she thought they'd done any good. Her answer was, "Well, lightning hasn't hit the house has it?"

In our case, it was fortunate I'd had the rods connected. Later that summer we were awakened in the middle of the night by a huge boom. We both sat up in bed, grabbed each other, and then checked to make sure the kids were okay. Our phone line was dead. Everyone got up and searched for evidence of fire. Thankfully there was none.

Once dawn came, we went outside and could see places where the earth was scorched as the lightning followed the phone line underground and up to the phone box on the side of the house, directly outside the head of our bed.

We eventually found the melted blob of what used to be the black plastic phone box cover about fifty feet away from the house.

We also discovered a small line of charred paint that went all the way around the house at the bottom of the steel siding. The house must have lit up like Times Square on New Year's Eve. It's a wonder we weren't all fried.

I have no idea if the ground rods helped in any way, but I was still glad I'd had them connected. There was never any telling when lightning might strike again.

Going for a Little Walk – August 1982

NOW THAT HAVEST was over, there were plenty of things to do, but nothing as hectic as June and July had been.

Most days I had time to take a walk from the house to the Baseline Road (a half mile) then east on the Baseline another half mile and then back to the house. A leisurely two-mile walk. At least, most days it was leisurely.

One afternoon I set off walking and talking to the red-winged blackbird that flew from one perch to another on the phone line and sang to me as we went along. Suddenly I spied a movement in the deep barrow ditch on the other side of the road. I stopped. Slowly, a monstrous dark brown bull—there was no doubt that he was a bull—rose from the ditch, swung his head toward me, and stared. I guess I'd interrupted his nap.

Oh shit. Should I stand still or run back to the house?

Neither of those options seemed to fit the situation. The only possible shelter was the telephone pole about thirty feet away.

Can I get there if he charges? And how long would I be able to run round and round that pole before he got me? For that matter, a bull could probably knock down a telephone pole without thinking twice about it.

My blackbird was still singing—easy for him; he wasn't on the ground.

I took a slow step toward the pole. Then another. The bull turned his head with my movement as I gingerly crept forward. Slow steps, listening for a snort—don't bulls always snort before they charge?—always keeping an eye on him but trying not to look him in the eye. No challenges from me.

I got to the pole and peeked out from behind it. He had turned around but hadn't moved from his spot in the ditch, so I kept on walking from pole to pole and then east on the Baseline Road—my usual route. All the while I kept looking behind me.

When I came back, the bull was gone.

I told Marvin about the encounter.

"That's Parker's bull."

Parker was one of our neighbors.

"But," Marvin added, "he's pretty old."

"Parker or the bull?"

He considered this. "Both, I think."

A few days later we were in the coffee shop in town and heard that the bull had died. I guess I scared him to death, but I didn't tell anyone about it for a long, long time.

An Entry at the County Fair

I SPENT A lot of time cooking. The calorie requirements of one farmer and one almost teen-age son were huge. Never before had I needed to produce such amounts of salads, meats, mashed potatoes, gravy, vegetables, and desserts. I needed better tools than the puny ones I was accustomed to using: bigger pots and pans; a Kitchen Aid mixer with attachments for grating, slicing, and grinding; a stronger blender; a pressure cooker; and canning equipment.

My sister-in-law Virginia taught me how to can pickles and tomatoes. I got a lot of practice as more and more of these two veggies ripened every day. One day, as I gathered cucumbers and dill weed, a huge grasshopper landed on my shoe—almost as if it were volunteering. Poof! I had an IDEA! I grabbed the grasshopper, put him in my shirt pocket, and buttoned the flap.

That morning I'd been reading the county fair booklet section on exhibitions and the judging process and had noticed they had a category for dill pickles.

I took my harvest inside and plunked the still-wiggling grasshopper in a jar of vinegar. He didn't wiggle very long. I prepared the cucumbers, put them in pint jars with sprigs of dill weed and my mixture of vinegar and spices. In the last jar I added a lot of salt as a preservative and inserted my grasshopper so that he looked out of the jar between two cucumbers. A sprig of dill behind him provided a bit of camouflage. Into the canning kettle went the jars, and I made a label with an ink drawing of a grasshopper, a cucumber, and the name "Hopper Dills."

I showed the jar to Marvin when he came in from the field.

"Are you really going to take those to the fair?"

"Well, yeah. It'll be good for a laugh or two."

He mumbled something.

I paused, then asked, "Is it okay with you?"

"Yeah, I guess."

On the designated day I presented my entry to the ladies in charge of the pickles, carefully pointing out the grasshopper and telling them that my recipe was based on an old one a great-great-grandmother had obtained while on a trip to North Africa decades ago. "You don't have to judge this jar," I said. "It's really just a joke."

At the rodeo that afternoon, lots of friends came up to me, laughing and congratulating me for doing something so different.

Apparently the ladies hadn't informed the judge not to taste my Hopper Dills. Not only had they been judged, they'd won third-place, even though they were the only entry in the Miscellaneous Division. The judge commented that they were "too salty." I guess that's why I wasn't given a first place.

I guess nobody got the joke—but I got a ribbon out of it.

Preparing the Fields for Planting

DURING AUGUST WE took turns tilling the fields to prepare them for planting wheat early in September. Sometimes we rode together in the tractor. Other times one of us rode alone while the other attended to the numerous duties that always awaited us.

At first, Marvin worked at cleaning and repairing all the things—machinery, vehicles, buildings, fences, bins—that had developed problems during the hectic first part of summer.

Then he began applying fertilizer to the fields. My job was to go get the tanks of anhydrous ammonia and pull them to the field where he was working or to the house for use the next day. I usually got two tanks at a time, hitching them in tandem behind the pickup.

Generally, someone was available to help me. If no one else was around the place, I had to do it myself, so I became very skilled at backing up so the hole in my pickup hitch was

directly beneath the hole in the tank hitch. Sometimes I had to climb on the bumper of the pickup and jump up and down to persuade the holes to line up so I could insert the pin that fastened everything together.

Each tank was about fifteen feet long, weighed about a ton when full, and contained one thousand gallons of liquid fertilizer. Though they look like bombs on wheels, they are not explosive. Still, anhydrous ammonia is dangerous stuff. Each tank carried a five-gallon tank of clean water for flushing eyes and skin in case of exposure to the chemical. I didn't think that was nearly enough.

On the way home I had to be especially careful approaching corners. Quick stops or turns were out of the question because the weight of the tanks pushed straight ahead against the pickup hitch. An object in motion stays in motion. If I didn't slow down soon enough, I would have to back up the two tanks without jack-knifing them—a tricky job I didn't want to attempt. I was extremely careful. If I missed the corner, I'd have to drive on the country roads for four long miles in a great wide square I order to get back to our farm.

When I hauled a tank into the field, we had to hook the tank to the implement that was hooked up to the tractor, then open the valve on the tank to let the anhydrous flow into the plastic tubes that worked their way to just behind the sweeps and close to the ground where the fertilizer flowed out into the furrows. During this operation we made sure we were upwind of the ammonia as much as possible. And hoped like everything the wind didn't shift.

I stayed with Marvin in the tractor as much as I could while he applied the anhydrous. Once in a while one or more of the tubes that fed the fertilizer to the ground would freeze up or get plugged with dirt. I turned off the valve to the tank while Marvin put on goggles and special rubber gloves to crawl under the implement to unplug the tube. Only, sometimes he was in too much of a hurry.

"Don't worry," he'd say as he crawled under the implement with only his regular work gloves and glasses. "I'll be careful."

Yeah, right, I thought as I stood there, scared to death and prepared to summon superwoman strength to drag him out in the open and dowse him, especially his face and eyes, with all five gallons of the clean water.

Here is a quote from *Nutrient Management: Using Anhydrous Ammonia Safely on a Farm*, a publication from the University of Minnesota Extension Agency:

> Special precautions are necessary when removing
> dirt from clogged applicator tubes. Because pressure
> can build up in the tubes if they become clogged, a
> rush of anhydrous ammonia can be expected when
> they are unclogged. Wear your goggles, gloves, and

a long-sleeved shirt while unclogging tubes. Position
yourself upwind from the clogged tube.
Darn stubborn man.

Sowing and Sewing – August and September 1982

IN LATE AUGUST we finished preparing the ground for our next wheat crop. I enjoyed the clean dirt smell and the deep, throaty song of the big tractor as I went over the ground, making beautiful loops at the edges of the fields. I watched the long-legged killdeer birds running alongside the tractor looking for overturned bugs to eat and hawks circling the sky, ready to pounce on any fieldmice the tractor exposed.

Conversation in the café was about varieties of wheat. I was the only woman in the group around one of the big tables.

"Well, I dunno," said Sam, "but I think Wichita® is still the best. What do you think, Marvin?"

"I've used Wichita for years and gotten pretty good crops, but the heads sure do shatter easily. I just hate to see all those kernels on the ground behind the combine."

Louis chimed in. "Yeah, it does shatter. What about some of the new varieties? Anybody know anything about them?"

"I've kinda been looking at Tam 107®," offered Rosco. "It's supposed to be more shatter-resistant, and the straw is easy to cut up. What about you, Marvin? You know anything?"

"Some. I read somewhere that it's drought and disease resistant." He shrugged. "But I guess the grasshoppers will like it just as much as Wichita."

"Yeah," chimed in several of the men at once. "Those grasshoppers always get their share."

Except for the one in my pickle jar, I thought.

The other guys stayed to discuss world-shaking events, but Marvin stood up. "I need to get to work. Catch ya later."

At home we checked the drills and repaired anything that had broken during the winter ice and snowstorms. We cleaned the seed boxes on the drills. We brought the bags of Tam 107 seed out from under the tarp where they'd been temporarily stored.

"When will you start planting?"

"You plant wheat when it's time."

That's not much help, Marvin, I thought. But knowing him, I waited for the important, helpful part.

"Through the years I've learned that September tenth is usually the right time. Before I start in a field, I check the moisture in the soil. Then I drill a little way, get out of the tractor, and make sure the seed is at the right depth to get moisture so it can grow."

I thought about that. "I guess it's like how I plant a garden. Some things a person just knows. But once in a while I have to replant something that didn't do well because I planted it too early and the seed rotted in the ground."

"Once I had to re-drill a half-section."

A section is one square mile, I thought. "That's a lot. Why, though, do you call it drilling instead of sowing or planting?"

"Because that's what Dad called it."

"Oh."

That night I looked it up in my *Webster's*. Sure enough, about the fourth definition down I discovered: *drill vt to sow (seeds) by dropping along a shallow furrow*. The entry also indicated a possible French derivation from the 1700s. Dad was right, and that was what we were about to do.

After all the hard work of the summer, it was time to drill the wheat that we would harvest the next year. The truck was full of seed-wheat. The drills had new points, and we were ready to start.

Yea! This is the last new thing I'll have to learn this year, I thought.

I was wrong.

Next morning the air was cool and the sun was bright as we headed to the first field. A perfect fall day for drilling wheat. Marvin led the way in the tractor with the drills hooked on behind. I followed in the red truck that was full of seed-wheat. To the side of the truck bed Marvin had attached an electric auger with a flexible hose to fill the drill boxes when they were getting low.

At the back of the implement were the packer wheels that pressed dirt around the seeds. At the end of each of the sections of the implement (the drills) there was a chain that ran from the packer wheels to a shaft that fed the seed from the seed boxes into flexible tubes that led to the furrows that the drill point had just made. The chains wouldn't turn if the packer wheels were clogged and not turning. Marvin checked everything and started toward the tractor.

"Come on," he said. "I need you to watch the chains. If they aren't turning, no seed is being planted. It leaves a bare spot in the field."

I climbed into what was called the girlfriend seat in the tractor and looked out the back window. Marvin throttled up, put the tractor in gear, and we were drilling wheat. The chains were turning at each section of the forty-foot-wide drill.

We traveled west down the long side of the field, turned a 180 and started back east, parallel to our first pass. It didn't take long for me to realize the wind-blown dust was obscuring my view out the back window.

"Honey, I can't see the chains."

"Not at all?"

"No." But then the wind shifted. "Oh, wait. Now I can see pretty well."

"Okay. Just do the best you can."

I was imagining a green-and-brown-striped field as I coped with gusty winds obliterating my view every now and then.

Back and forth we went across the mile-long field for an hour or so.

"Um, a chain came off!"

He stopped to fix the chain.

"Just in time," I said. "My morning coffee is coming through."

"So is mine." His feet hit the ground. I got out, squatted in the shade of a big tractor wheel on the side farthest from the road, and pondered the immense solitude of the rest of the field, while he quickly got rid of his coffee and unclogged the packer wheels. The wind soon dried me off, and we climbed back into the tractor. Throttle up. Back and forth we went—chatting about our kids, family stories, and folks we knew in town.

"We better check the feed boxes," Marvin said as he stopped at the end of the field near our red truck.

I got out and followed him to the back of the drill where we stepped up on the narrow walkway to open the boxes and check the seed levels. They were getting low, so I trotted over to the truck, brought it even with the drills, engaged the hydraulic drive and lifted the truck box so Marvin could refill the drill with the auger. As soon as I moved the truck out of the way, off we went again.

We could receive only two radio stations: country music and Rush Limbaugh. What I would have given for Chopin or Rachmaninoff!

When I had things that had to be done in house or in town, Marvin watched the chains and filled the seed boxes himself. I think he just wanted me along for company. On the last day of planting, he asked me to come help. I had a different job this time.

"I want to use up all the seed in the boxes, so we won't have so much to clean out," he said. "It's easier to plant it than to clean it out with tin cans. We can't leave any in the boxes because it'll sprout or get moldy, and then it makes a mess. I'd rather run it out on the field."

That makes sense, I thought.

"I'll be going real slow now, and the lids on the boxes will be open, so you need to stand on the boards at the back and keep the seed levels even in the boxes. Just use your hands to push it around to keep it level.

I lost him at "… you need to stand on the boards at the back."

"Do what?"

He repeated himself.

"Um, what if I fall off?"

"I'll stop so you can get back on."

"Oh."

So I grabbed my gloves out of my back pocket, climbed up and held on while he started, then walked back and forth from one side of the implement to the other, keeping the seed level. Once I got used to it, I decided it was kind of fun—better than just sitting in the cab. Marvin was true to his word—he did go slowly. And I didn't fall off.

It took about a week to get all the fields drilled. In another week or so, we began to see it sprouting. How beautiful it was to look down the rows when the sun was low and see the tiny green shoots of our next crop poking up in the furrows. The wheat would go dormant through the winter, then green up next spring. It grew, ripened, and was ready to cut by early July.

The heavy work season was finished. We cleaned the drills and tractor. Now we could rest.

~ ~ ~

ONE MORNING, AFTER the kids had gone to school, our phone rang, and Marvin answered it. "I just put some cinnamon rolls in the oven," Mommy said. "Do you want some?"

"We'll be there as soon as we can. Honey," he hollered, "get your jacket on. We're going to town. Mommy's making cinnamon rolls!"

The heavenly scent met us at the front door as she took the first batch out of the oven. The are no cinnamon rolls anywhere in the world better than the ones Mommy made.

As the three of us sat around her table munching and talking, she mentioned she was going to her quilting circle the next afternoon. "Would you like to go with me?"

"Oh, I don't know if you want me there," I told her. "I know how to sew, but I've never done any quilting."

"Well, it's time you learned."

So that settled that.

The next afternoon I began my quilting career. Mommy had brought extra needles and thread for me. The group—all in their sixties and seventies and eighties—was going to start work on one of Mommy's quilts, so I got to learn how to put a quilt top, batting, and lining in the quilting frame. We rolled this "sandwich" carefully onto one of the side rails while the other side was safety-pinned to a strip of fabric on the opposite rail. The rails rested on sawhorses built by the husbands and carefully sized for our purpose. We took our seats at the two rails and began to stitch the "sandwich" together, carefully following the pattern with small tidy stitches.

We stitched and talked.

"How do you like living on a farm?" Julia asked me.

"I love it. Marvin's been teaching me how to run all the machinery. I really like the tractor the most."

They gave me some strange glances.

"The only really hard part in harvest is when I have to sit in a truck out in the field waiting to get a full load. The flies try to chew me up. The combine is fun, but mostly I help the truck drivers dump their loads. I run the auger and keep track of the loads—which field, the number of bushels. All that kind of stuff."

"You do all that?" Ellen arched her eyebrows in surprise. They all stared at me.

"You're not supposed to do that," Cora added. "You're supposed to stay in the house and cook."

I thought about that. "Well, our custom cutters take care of their own meals, so all I have to do is provide for our family—Erica always spends the summers with her dad, so it's just the three of us. I usually make sandwiches for lunch and casseroles or stew for supper—things that don't take much time, and I always keep some meals in the freezer in case we need them."

The silence was deafening for just a moment.

Was I really breaking some farm wife code I didn't know about?

But the hum of friendly gossip returned—who'd gotten married, who'd gone on a trip, how grandchildren were doing in school. I hoped Mommy wasn't embarrassed by what I'd said, so when we got back to her house I asked her about it.

"Humph," she snorted. "Don't you worry about a thing. When I was young my father didn't have any boys, so I was his helper. He called me his *boy*. And there are a lot of women around here who do field work. They just don't like it the way you do."

What wasn't to like?

All that work for such a satisfying result.

And the companionship of working with the man I loved.

Sort of like putting a quilt together with my beloved mother-in-law.

Thanksgiving Dinner – November 1982

SOON AFTER OUR wedding the previous March, one of my new sisters-in-law (Ilene) had made a comment about how the newest woman in the family always had to make Thanksgiving dinner.

"Sure," I'd said without a second thought.

I'd made plenty of turkey dinners with the guidance of an article, "The Bride Makes Thanksgiving Dinner," that I'd clipped from a women's magazine from way back when I was married the first time at the age of twenty. No sweat.

So, with the holiday approaching I invited Mommy, Marvin's mother; Virginia, Marvin's elder sister, and her husband Eldred; Walter, Marvin's brother, and Ilene his wife, who had lived next door to me in Denver; Sarah, Marvin's other sister, and Ron, her husband; and my parents, who would drive up from Colorado Springs. With Marvin, myself, three children, and two grandchildren that made sixteen people. A big crowd for sure, but I didn't think it would be too hard. Big mistake.

What I didn't know was that inviting Marvin's brother and sisters and their spouses meant their children and grandchildren were also invited. My list swelled to twenty-six people. I flew into a panic.

"How," I demanded of Marvin, "am I going to cook a meal for that many people?"

"Don't worry. Everybody brings something. You just have to do the turkey, dressing, gravy, and potatoes."

"We don't even have seating for them all. The dining room table only seats ten, and that's with both leaves in. And dishes! We don't have enough place settings."

"Honey, it's all going to be okay. There are extra dishes and stuff in a box downstairs. Don't worry."

Fine for him to say. He wouldn't have to do the cooking.

"I'm going to need a huge turkey, or even if I get two smaller ones, they won't both fit in the oven, and I don't even have a roasting pan big enough."

"Mommy has an electric roasting pan that will hold the biggest turkey you can find, and they always come out nice and moist. Don't worry," he repeated. "That's how we always do it."

"Where are we going to get more tables, and where will we put them? And chairs—what about chairs?"

"We borrow them from the Methodist Church social hall. The men always handle that part. Two pickup loads is all it takes."

"Yeah, but…" I started.

"Virginia brings her special fruit salad. Mommy brings pies." Then he rattled on about green beans, sweet potatoes, cranberry sauce, and more. By the end of his list he was positively drooling.

"Oh," I said, not quite believing him.

I called Virginia, and she assured me that what he said was true.

The preparations went as Marvin had said they would. The men set up the tables. Somebody brought the plates from the basement and washed them all ahead of time. People came with their promised dishes—the cold ones were cold and the hot ones were hot. In the kitchen, Mommy and Virginia watched over the turkey. Marvin and my daddy mashed the potatoes. Ilene and I made the gravy. The children helped by filling the water and iced tea glasses. My in-laws knew their jobs, having participated in this ritual many times.

~ ~ ~

AFTER DINNER, WE all sat around talking about family genealogy. I was reminded of my college anthropology professor who taught us that when two aboriginal Australians meet, they determine their kinship ties back many generations to find out which moiety, one of two basic tribal subdivisions, they belong to. It had something to do with marriageability.

"Has anybody heard from Aunt Mable lately?"

"Last I heard, her daughter married a man from Alaska, but that was quite a while ago."

"Is that the daughter who used to be married to Homer Smith over in Yuma?"

"No, I think that was her third daughter with Francis Perry when they lived in Burlington."

And so on. The conversation ebbed and flowed with everybody joining in with their own opinions of who was married to whom, who had died or moved or married or divorced, and even whose offspring were in jail. Eventually, family photo albums and scrapbooks were brought out for perusal.

We also shared family stories. Eldred told of the time he worked a field along the Baseline Road near a small stand of trees. "I noticed some hunters there but didn't think too much about it until I heard a shot. At the same time I felt something hit the middle of my forehead and blood draining down my face. I knew for sure I'd been shot and wondered why I wasn't already dead. I grabbed a rag real quick to wipe my eyes and discovered that a line had burst, and hydraulic fluid had spurted right onto the middle of my forehead. I wasn't dead after all."

"That reminds me of the scar on Marvin's forehead," said Sarah. "Daddy told us kids to move the scrap iron pile farther away from the shop, so Walter and I decided to throw the pieces to their new location. Marvin was too little to throw them, so he was carrying the ones he could lift. Walter accidentally threw one that hit Marvin in the head. *Don't tell Mommy, don't tell Mommy*, he cried—until he saw the blood running down Marvin's face. *Go get Mommy,* he yelled. *Go get Mommy!*"

~ ~ ~

SUCH FAMILY STORIES were appreciated and retold at many family dinners. Of course, weather, crops, and government farm programs were always topics for farmers, retired farmers, and up-and-coming farmers.

Through future years I became more integrated into the teamwork of the family, acting as hostess sometimes and as helper other times. The main point was that we all worked together and enjoyed each other's company.

"Hooding" in the Pasture – December 1982

WINTER ARRIVED WITH howling winds and snow blowing sideways. Scott and Erica were delighted there would be no school the next day. Their dreams were dashed however, when Marvin reminded them that we lived at the end of the school bus route, and the snowplows would soon arrive plowing a nice path on the driveway all the way around our house, so the school bus could get through.

Sure enough. At six o'clock the next morning the snowplow driver grinned and waved as he made two passes through the five-foot-high drifts. The school bus wasn't far behind him—not at all like Denver where school was cancelled when only a few inches of snow had fallen.

This snow was different from the deep powder snow I'd been accustomed to when I lived in Steamboat Springs. Here, the wind created hard-packed drifts that looked like layers of wind-sculpted sandstone.

That weekend, after the wind stopped blowing, we found the pasture was coated with four or five inches of snow, but only a few drifts. "We can go hooding," Marvin announced with a big smile.

"Yeah!" shouted Scott.

"What's hooding?" Erica and I asked at the same time.

"Get your warm clothes on, and you'll see."

We all scrambled to get dressed—long underwear, turtlenecks, sweaters, coveralls, and jackets, caps, and gloves. We went to the horse barn where we dug through a drift to open the door. Marvin disappeared inside. After some noise of metal things being shuffled around, he appeared dragging an old car hood and carrying an armful of tattered blankets and feed sacks.

"Scott," he said, "you can ride first to show them how it works."

As Marvin fastened a rope between the hood and the hitch on the pickup, Scott arranged the blankets in the upside-down hood. "It's so my knees won't get hurt," he explained.

Marvin climbed into the pickup and hollered, "Ready?"

Scott grabbed the front edge of the hood with both hands and yelled, "Go!"

Away they went across the pasture with Scott grinning and getting a face full of snow.

The four of us spent a wonderful morning zipping back and forth, taking turns driving and riding. We finally got tired and headed back to the house for lunch. When I went into the bathroom and looked in the mirror, my face was brown with the dirt that had flown up with the snow. Then I realized it wasn't just dirt. There were cow pies all over that pasture!

The Rest of Winter – 1982-1983

AFTER THE HECTIC schedule of the previous months, the rest of winter was truly a time of rest, relaxation, fun, and friendship. The kids went to school. Scott played on the junior-high basketball team, and Erica was busy making good friends.

We went to basketball games and attended Saturday night dances in the basement of the V.F.W. There was still a movie theater in town, so we enjoyed movies with the kids. Sometimes we drove to Denver or Colorado Springs to visit relatives. Marvin's mother (Mommy) went with us on these trips. When we hadn't visited with her recently, she'd get lonely and call us to announce that a fresh batch of cinnamon rolls would be coming out of the oven soon. No matter what the weather was, we quickly got to her house in town.

The pasture became a place for driving lessons when the snow melted a little and froze again. It was a huge ice rink with nothing to run into. Erica would turn sixteen the following summer and get her driver's license. Scott could already drive but needed practice. Marvin's goal was to teach them to drive in slick conditions. He took them one at a time in the pickup and taught them how to recover from a skid. First, he demonstrated the maneuver, then coached as they practiced intentionally going into a skid and getting out of it. The kids loved these sessions and are still good winter drivers.

Marvin's niece and her family came from Fort Morgan with their snowmobiles and two giant inner tubes. We didn't stay in the flat part of the pasture this time. The intermittent creek with its twists, turns, and high banks hadn't had water in it since summer. Now it was covered with snow. Each snowmobile had an inner tube tied behind it with a long, long rope. The driver would get up speed and then suddenly turn away from the creek where the banks were highest, causing the person on the inner tube to swing over the bank and into the creek bed, where they upset, yelling and laughing the whole time.

Sometimes there was nothing to do, so we went to town and joined other farmers and their wives at the coffee shop. The talk was about the year's government farm programs; advances in farm equipment and how expensive it would be; which varieties of wheat would do best; and, of course, the weather. Then there was local gossip, politics, and cattle mutilations. About half the people thought the mutilations were done by aliens, and the other half thought the government was responsible. These conversations were conducted over pie, cinnamon rolls (not quite as good as Mommy's), and coffee.

On the way home one afternoon, I asked Marvin if any of his cattle had been mutilated.

"I don't know," he said. "I found two steers once—one on each side of the creek. Each one weighed about eight hundred pounds and looked like it had been shoved with a lot of force into a depression where the water had made an undercut in the bank of the stream. I couldn't find any tracks in the dirt or any blood or missing parts, so I just called the dead cow truck to come get them. Maybe I should have reported it, but I didn't figure anything would come of it."

Marvin and I planned for the coming farming season and on warmer days fixed a few fences just to stay in shape and get a head start on spring work.

One of my decisions involved the garden. I decided not to plant so many vegetables—especially green beans. The garden work the previous summer had been too much, and one day in the grocery store I noticed the price of green beans. I figured out the store-bought ones were way cheaper than the cost of raising, harvesting, and canning or freezing the ones from the garden—especially so, considering the value of my time, which I thought should equal, at least, that of a bookkeeper or truck driver.

Then I remembered the perks that went with my farm wife job: living on the majestic prairie, enjoying my new extended family, sleeping with the owner, and sharing in the profits.

Those things counted for a lot. But I still didn't plant green beans anymore.

Hauling Wheat to the Elevator – January 1983

ONE EVENING AS we were sitting in our chairs watching TV, Marvin announced we'd be hauling wheat to town starting the next day. I noticed that he used the word *we*.

Somehow, it had never occurred to me that all that wheat we'd put into the bins and the big Quonset, the round-top, would eventually have to be taken out and transported to the grain elevator in town.

"I always sell wheat in January," he said, "because the price is usually better than right after harvest."

"Oh," I replied. "How long will it take?"

"I try to get six loads a day, but usually I can do only five. It takes a lot of time to load the truck, tarp it down, drive it to the elevator, dump the wheat, and come back home."

"What will I be doing?"

"We'll use the long auger inside the round-top. You can manage the red truck and keep an eye on how the load is distributed. You might have to shovel some of the wheat around in the bed of the truck to keep the load even and back the truck up as I move the auger farther back into the wheat."

"Okay." It sounded simple enough.

Earlier in the month, Marvin had insisted that we go to the big farm-supply store in Fort Morgan to buy coveralls and a stocking cap for me. "It's going to be really cold the next couple of months," he'd said by way of explanation. Now I knew why I needed them.

The next morning, I put my new outfit on over my jeans, turtleneck, and sweater and went with Marvin to move the auger into the round-top. We used the small tractor to push the low end of the auger into the pile of wheat while being sure the top end would clear the truck bed.

"That's good," Marvin yelled at me as I maneuvered the truck into the right spot.

He turned on the power take-off, the auger began to turn, and the wheat began to pour into the truck.

[*Editor's Note: This photo looks approximately like the one they used except that Marvin's auger was twice as long—forty feet long.*]

When the truck was loaded, I helped Marvin scoop the small piles of grain that the auger had missed back onto the pile. Then we tarped the truck—just a matter of cranking the roller arrangement Marvin had invented and then tying down the tarp edges so it wouldn't flap in the wind—and headed to the elevator.

We chatted until we got to a long, gentle incline and began picking up speed. At the bottom of the hill was a forty-five-degree left turn. Marvin applied the brakes. The pedal went all the way to the floor!

"Damn, we don't have any brakes!"

"Oh, shit," was all I could think to say.

"Yeah," he growled.

He geared down and down and down until the truck was in the lowest gear, the engine screaming at us. I braced myself with feet and hands, but using the emergency brake, Marvin managed to get us stopped after we'd gone a little way off the road into softer dirt.

"Oh shit," I repeated.

"Yeah," he replied.

He managed somehow to back out of the dirt, shifted into first gear, and went around the corner. Needless to say, we sighed in big relief. It wouldn't have been fun if the truck had sunk into the dirt up to its axles.

To get to the elevator we had to go about five hundred more yards, then around a right-hand corner of the road, and into an immediate left-hand turn at the elevator's driveway. As he pulled the truck onto the scale, Marvin again used the emergency brake to stop.

I was surprised to see that our truck was sitting on top of fat steel bars that stretched between the left and right side of the scale. There were gaps between the bars so the wheat could flow into the pit below. Later I learned that an augur in the bottom of the pit—what would farms ever do without those contraptions?—moved the wheat into the tall silos for storage. On the other side of the silos was a train siding where the wheat could be loaded into hopper cars when the elevator sold the wheat into the world market.

After we removed the tarp from the truck, the man at the grain elevator climbed up and inserted a probe into the wheat.

"Why's he doing that?"

"He'll test that sample for moisture content to find the weight per bushel and the amount of protein in it. If the wheat's too wet, it'll spoil in the elevator. Sixty pounds per bushel is about the right weight. That works out to twelve or thirteen percent moisture. He also tests for protein content. A high protein content will bring us a much better price."

"Oh," I said. *Clear as mud.*

I was about to ask how the elevator man would know how much wheat we had, but Marvin started climbing out of the truck.

"Can I come, too??

"Sure."

Marvin introduced me to Walt, the elevator man, and then he headed straight to the bathroom.

I had more questions, but when Marvin came out of the bathroom, he and Walt began chatting.

"Doesn't look like you're very busy today," Marvin said.

"Nope. Not many people hauling. Most of them brought their wheat at harvest."

It was my turn to use the bathroom.

Eventually Marvin said, "Well, I guess we better unload. Wouldn't want to delay anyone else who might show up."

Walt walked to the back of the truck and opened the big door that let the wheat flow out. Marvin got in the driver's seat, engaged the hydraulics, and raised the truck bed. I saw a golden waterfall gushing out of the truck through the boards into the pit.

When the truck was empty, Walt signaled Marvin to lower the bed. I climbed into the passenger seat. Walt weighed us again and gave us the grain receipt. Our wheat had lots of protein.

On the way back home, Marvin used only the gears to brake. Uphill wasn't nearly as scary, but he still had to take care when we went around corners.

"I've got to repair the brake line and add fluid before we can do another load," he said as we turned into the drive and headed toward the shop.

"Honey, would you let me off at the house?"

"Why?"

"To do the same thing you got to do at the elevator."

"Why didn't you go there?"

"The bathroom was too small for me to get far enough out of my coveralls. Besides it was freezing in there, and I wasn't about to sit down on that dirty thing." Men had it so easy.

"Oh," he said.

I did my duty, washed up, set out some leftovers to thaw for supper that night, and went out to help Marvin repair the brake line.

We managed only two more loads that day.

"How long will it take us to get all the wheat to town?" I asked during the next trip.

"About ten days, but we won't be taking all of it. I've been holding some back each year in case we have a bad yield the next couple of years. I just haul enough wheat to pay the farm expenses and personal bills until the next year."

First he gets us a higher price per bushel by waiting well after harvest, and then he plans ahead for the possibility of lean years. Sharp as a tack, that man!

Calving Cows – Late Winter/Early Spring 1983

WE WATCHED THE other farmers' pastures as the cows began to drop their calves.

"See those calves kind of bunched up together taking a nap?" Marvin pointed. "There's only one cow with them. She's the babysitter. The other cows are grazing farther away and will come back when the calves start waking up."

I was skeptical. "How do they know who's going to babysit? And why don't the calves follow their mothers?"

"I guess they have their own cow way of knowing when it's their turn to babysit." Marvin squinted at the bundle of babies. "Their mothers told them to stay, so they stayed. The cows are like other animal mothers—deer, antelope, bears, cougars. They hide their babies and tell them to stay put while they go find food for themselves or to take home to the babies if they're meat-eaters."

He slowed as we came to another pasture. "Look there, beside that fence post."

There lay a tiny Hereford calf—probably a newborn—barely visible, peering out over dry grass clumps.

"Where's the mother?"

We looked around. "There she is." Marvin pointed to a cow about two hundred feet from the calf. "That calf will stay right there unless somebody spooks it. If that happens, it'll take off and run until it drops. If the mother can't find it, it'll die."

At home in my basement studio I made a colored pencil drawing of that new calf by the fence post. I named it *Baby Hiding* and sold it to a woman who gave it to her husband as a birthday present. It still hangs in his office in Sterling, Colorado.

~ ~ ~

THE NEXT DAY brought wind and snow. "Isn't it hard on the calves to plop out into this freezing weather?" I asked. "Do a lot of them die?"

"The mothers are inseminated," Marvin explained, "so the calves will be at the right weight when the market demand is high. It had nothing to do with the convenience of the cows or calves. I tried to time mine to calve in March when it's a little warmer, but if there was low atmospheric pressure or bad weather coming, that's when they'd drop their calves."

His face took on a pensive look. "If the forecast was bad, I put the cows in the corrals so I could keep watch over them. I had to make sure each mother licked her calf dry so it wouldn't freeze. Sometimes she'd abandon her calf. If a calf wasn't doing well—standing up, walking around, and nursing—I picked it up and took it into the house."

"Inside the house?"

"Yeah. They were damn slippery little things."

"How much did they weigh?"

"Oh, I guess about eighty-five pounds or so. I had to get it warmed up and dry so it wouldn't die on us, so I'd put it next to the floor furnace and dry it off with rags."

"Yuck," I said. "Didn't you get all that slimy stuff all over you?"

"Yeah, but that was good because when the calf could finally stand up on its own, I had to pick it up and take it back to the corral. The mother would smell her scent on me as well as on the calf, and she'd come get it—the calf, not me."

"Oh." I said *Oh* a lot while I was learning about being a farm wife. I thought about this new-found calf knowledge a little while. "Now that I think about it, I'm pretty sure I could smell Erica when she was born, or maybe, probably, it was my scent on her, but then the delivery room people took her away. When they finally brought her to me, she was all cleaned up and smelled like soap."

I pondered a bit longer. "Looking back at the experience, I wish I could have held her right away."

Verne's Cows – Spring 1983

THE WHEAT BEGAN waking up from its winter dormancy. Frogs began to croak, and the meadow larks returned with their beautiful song. Geese honked as they flew north, stopping overnight at our small pond.

We fixed fences and checked the grass to be sure there would be plenty for the cows that would soon be brought to our pasture. Marvin cleaned the stock tank in the big pasture then climbed the windmill and turned it on. Water began flowing into the tank.

The cows that year didn't belong to the same owner as the herd we had the previous year. These came in two semi-truckloads and bolted as soon as they were unloaded and found their calves. After a few days they figured out where the windmill, stock tanks, ponds, and fences were located. And the lead cow quickly found a low place in the fence. Plenty of grass grew in our pasture, but she led the other cows over the fence and across the Baseline Road to a neighbor's field of hershey (a type of millet) that had just come up. Marvin and I drove over there in the pickup and chased her back over the fence, the other cows following her.

We pulled the top wire of the fence higher.

A few days later Marvin saw the lead cow moving toward the fence. "Come quick, Honey," he yelled—the clarion call to action. "I'm going to teach her a lesson."

I jumped in the pickup and away we went bouncing across the deep cow paths worn in the prairie soil. He got behind that cow and turned her away from the fence.

"You damn bitch," he yelled and got close enough behind her that the back hooves hit the front bumper as she ran. Every time she tried to turn toward the fence, he swerved to the side and ran her away from it. This battle of wills went on and on, with the tires churning up a spray of dirt, the pickup overheating, and Marvin yelling, "You damn bitch. Where do you think you're going? I'll make hamburger out of you. You damn bitch."

I was holding on for dear life until the cow tired and quit trying to run to the fence. I sure was glad Marvin wasn't the kind of man who'd teach his wife a lesson that way! But with a stubborn lead cow, it had sure been necessary. For the rest of that summer, he called all those cows "you damn bitches."

Later that summer Marvin and I were riding around the pasture checking fences. I asked him why he hated cows so much; he was always complaining about them.

"I don't hate cows," he said. "Just other people's cows. When I had my own herd, I lived here on the place and so did they, so they knew it was home. They didn't get out of the pasture, didn't tear down fences, didn't kick hell out of the corrals. These people who rent the pasture now—they move their cows all the time, take them to cornstalks, move them here and there, and the cows never learn where home is—because they don't *have* a home. That's why they try to get out all the time."

Taking them to cornstalks, by the way, involved putting up an electric fence around the corn field after the corn was harvested, loading the cows into trucks, unloading them within the fenced enclosure, and then sixty days later reversing the process to take them back to the first pasture and start the calving. It's a process that's incredibly hard on the cows.

"Before I ran cow-calf pairs," Marvin explained, "I bought calves. I'd feed them every morning and walk around the herd and talk to them. By the time spring came and it was time to turn them out to pasture, they knew this was their home. Young'uns," he added, "adapt better than adults."

We were quiet for a while, and then he resumed. "One year there was a blizzard and the cows went through the fence and drifted away south. They turned their back ends to the wind and drifted with it. When the storm was over, I went out and spent half a day looking for them. Never found even one, but that afternoon they all came walking up the road. I opened the gate and they went into the corral, hungry and thirsty. They knew where to go to get fed. They knew where home was."

He pointed at the uprooted herd munching on our pasture grass. "These ladies wouldn't have lasted through a blizzard like that, because they wouldn't have known where to go."

It was a sobering thought.

The Cows Get Out Again

I WAS HOME alone working on a quilt when Erica returned from town where she'd spent the night with a friend. I heard her honking the horn as she sped into the drive and skidded to a stop at the kitchen door.

"Mom! The cows are jumping over the fence and going to that millet field across the Baseline Road! I could see them from the corner."

"Meet me at the Jeep," I shouted and ran for the back door, the quickest route to the shop where we parked the Jeep. I got there first, started it up, then met her halfway between the shop and the house. She jumped in and away we went to the Baseline Road and the millet field. Those damn bitches were munching away like crazy—on our neighboring farmer's millet crop.

What should I do? "Do we get out and try to herd them to the fence? Or use the pickup that will tear up even more of the hershey?" I didn't have to think about it very long.

"Erica, you use the Jeep to keep them from going into the other fields. I'll chase them into the pasture."

I bailed out and started running, waving my arms, my long hair flapping in the wind, trying to make them go back to where they belonged, screaming, "You damn bitches, you damn bitches," the whole time. The lead cow must have remembered her previous lesson from Marvin when he chased her with the pickup, or maybe she thought I was some crazed creature from another world, because it didn't take them long to jump back over the fence.

When they were back where they belonged—within the confines of the fence—Erica picked me up. We waited quite a while until the cows finally meandered to the other side of the pasture.

As we started back to the house, Erica said, "Mom, I never knew you talked like that."

Truth was, I never used to—until I met those damn … er … those particular bovines.

Cleaning the Stock Tank – Summer 1983

"HONEY, COME HELP me clean out the stock tank," he said. "It won't take long." I could tell this was another one of those moments that justified his having taught me to keep my shoes on in the house. I was ready to go as soon as I heard his call.

I grabbed my work gloves and followed him to the pickup where we loaded a couple of rakes and set out toward the stock tank.

We drove to the pasture gate by the corrals where I got out and held the gate open while he drove through. Then I shut the gate and got back in the pickup. We drove a mile through the pasture to the stock tank where we found a layer of green moss on the water around the rim of the tank. It extended four or five feet toward the center, and there were some green patches in the middle.

"You start raking the moss out of the tank while I shut the windmill off," Marvin said. "Then I'll come help.

"Will the cows eat this?" I yelled at his disappearing back.

"No," came the reply. "It'll just rot."

Seems like a waste, I thought, but I'd already started raking around the edges and throwing the moss away from the tank onto the mud around it. Holding up the end of the rake out in the water was difficult—those tines were heavy. When Marvin came back from the windmill, I had an idea.

"Go over to the other side," I directed. "I'll stay on this side and make waves so the water will carry the moss to your side where you can pull it out. Your arms are longer and stronger than mine."

We worked like this, moving around the perimeter until a single cow came over the hill and headed toward the north side of the tank. I was on the south side, and Marvin was halfway between me and the cow. We stopped working. The cow came to the edge of the tank, lowered her head over the water, and looked at me. I lowered my head over the water and looked back at her. She took a drink, still looking at me. I got a silly notion and stuck my tongue out at her, whereupon she threw up her head, turned, and galloped back up the hill, bag swinging between her hind legs. I bet her calf had buttermilk that afternoon.

Wheat Harvest—Ooops! – July 1983

THE COMBINE, THAT monster that cut the wheat, captured the wheat kernels, and blew the chaff back onto the land, went round and round the field. When the combine bin was full of wheat Marvin angled the unloading auger out over the bed of a truck which had moved up alongside the combine, pushed a button, and the auger rumbled a torrent of wheat into the truck. When the truck was full, Marvin pulled the auger back in and cut more wheat. Cut wheat and unload. Listen and diagnose all the noises of this combined collection of machinery. Watch the sky. Cut wheat and unload. Listen and watch the sky. Cut wheat and unload. Long days.

Scott took a loaded truck to the house. Marvin dumped a bin full on my red truck, and we paused a moment eyeing the storm that was building on the horizon, gauging the wind, figuring out which way it would move. Was there time for him to cut another bin full? Then we felt a drop. Another drop. Another.

"No time to tarp the load," he yelled over the sudden gust of wind. "Get it home!"

The red truck groaned as I headed out of the field up onto the dirt road. "Oh, please," I prayed as I ran up through the gears of the old hi-lo transmission. "Please don't get slick." I approached the turn onto road JJ and shifted down through the gears. The road was slick, but I only slid a little. Geared up, then geared down for the turn into our driveway. At last I was in the yard and making the straight shot toward the round-top through the big double doors. By that time the rain was getting serious, and thunder was rolling.

Scott's truck was already safely inside. Marvin, right behind me on the combine, pulled into the double-doored shop building next to the round-top. Scott and I ran to the side of the round-top to crank the auger higher as Marvin climbed the curved ladder welded to the side of the round-top, danced along the top of the building to the hatch where we'd been dumping wheat, and closed the lid. *Please don't let him be hit by lightning.* Scott lowered the auger to hold the lid in place. No time to bolt it down properly.

I grabbed the tarp to cover the container around the lower end of the auger and placed the nearby cinderblocks to weight down the edges. Marvin ran to close and latch the shop doors. Scott and I did the same to the round-top doors.

Then we all ran for the house, laughing, exultant.

The next day we could have slept late, knowing we wouldn't be able to cut until the wheat dried out. Even so, we woke with too little rest, donned our clothes, grabbed some coffee, and went outside. Marvin grabbed his grease gun and began greasing the zerks (non-farmers call them grease nipples) on the combines. When he finished, he'd head to the school section and start cutting.

I went to warm up the little tractor that ran the auger, and Scott brought the red truck to the dumping station at the bottom end of the long auger that lifts the wheat up into the open hatch on top of the round-top. Looking in the rear-view mirror, watching my signals, my gangly teenaged son neatly backed the truck, centering the back end precisely over the bottom end of the auger. I turned on the auger and opened the unloading gate in the back of the truck. The gold river of wheat began to run. Scott engaged the hydraulics and lifted the truck bed a little. He emerged from the cab, stretched, yawned, then abruptly charged toward me yelling "Shut it off! Shut it off!"

I glanced over my shoulder to see what was wrong. "Oh, shit!" That river of gold was cascading not into the round-top, but down its rounded side, piling up on the weedy ground. I grabbed the lever to close the chute, then dove to turn off the auger. We'd forgotten to open the hatch!

We looked at each other in panic—a teenager and a woman who hadn't been raised on a farm. Now what do we do?

"Raise the auger," Scott shouted as he ran for the building. "I'll climb up and open the lid."

I raised the auger, grabbed the scoop shovel leaning against a tractor tire and started carrying the grain one shovel-full at a time from the pile beside the round-top to the dumping station. My brain was whirling. *Hurry! No, not so fast, you're spilling the wheat. Careful, don't fill the shovel so full. What's Marvin going to say? I know what he'll say—Well, whudjadothatfor?* That was what he always said when one of us messed up.

Scott and I scrambled about trying to clean up the grain together until we realized we hadn't emptied the truck yet.

"Geez! Dad's going to need it," Scott yelled.

I cranked the auger down again into the hatch, started it, and opened the unloading gate. Let 'er rip! But by that time the heavy truck bed had settled back into its original position, not high enough to let the wheat slip out the back. Scott started the truck and lifted the bed. At last the grain was flowing the way it should—into the bin.

As soon as the truck was empty, Scott headed for the field, not bothering to clean out the corners. I went back to cleaning up the spilled wheat, trying to get rid of the evidence.

Then I remembered the *other* full truck was still in the round-top.

"Oh, damn." I'd forgotten about the blue truck—the larger of the two. During harvest it was usually loaded with 650 bushels and took a long time to dump. Getting it out of the round-top in reverse was easy, but I hadn't mastered the thirteen forward gears, so I lurched slowly to the dumping station in granny gear—the lowest one. I backed in and had the blue truck half empty when Scott returned with another load. We just laughed about our mishap.

When the blue truck was empty, he drove off, and I dumped the red truck. Finally, things were in rhythm again, so I went back to getting rid of the evidence of our mistake. Picking up a shovel-full of wheat is hard to do when it's mixed with grass and dirt. I tried my best—even picking out the wheat kernels with my hands. I thought I'd done a pretty good job.

Nope.

When Marvin got home in the evening he came to see how we were doing with the last truck load of the day. He glanced around, spotted the remainder of the spilled grain, and asked, "What happened here?"

The man has eyes like a hawk! At least he didn't say *whudjadothatfor* this time.

Mommy's Pies – August 1983

A YEAR HAD passed since I'd taken my *Hopper Dills* to the Washington County Fair, and I'd become friends with many of the townspeople. I think they were still a bit wary of me, though. One friend, Betty, even told me I would always be known as a stranger because I was from a big city, and even worse, I was an artist. For this fair I decided not to make anything silly, and just entered loaves of white and whole wheat bread. My mother had taught me how to bake white bread when I was a young teenager, and I still used her original recipe.

My whole wheat bread was a combination from many recipes I'd acquired during the years. Many years ago I'd entered a loaf in the county fair in Routt County, Colorado, and won a blue ribbon for it. I hoped I'd win another one this year, but alas, the judges decided otherwise.

Mommy won blue ribbons for her cherry, apple, and strawberry-rhubarb pies. These awards were nothing new for her. She'd won blue or red ribbons almost every year and had a perennial competition with two other women to see which one would get the most blue ribbons. These women, now in their seventies and eighties, had been friends longer than I'd been alive, and each one had decades of practice at making pies.

When the time came to pick up the pies after the judging, Marvin and I and Virginia and Eldred drove into town and took Mommy to lunch before we went to the fairground with her to help her transport her pies home. Of course, we did want to be helpful, but the real reason was that she always invited us to stay for a serving (or two or three) of pie!

Separating Calves from the Cows – Late Summer 1983

A WEEK BEFORE, Marvin and Verne, the owner of the cows, had toured the pastures checking the grass and concluded it was time to move the cows. The grass was going into winter dormancy, and the cows couldn't get enough nutrition. If they were left in the pasture, they could damage the grass beyond recovery.

I knew it had to be done, but I hated the thought of it. Taking babies away from their mothers just didn't seem right, even if those babies had grown until they now weighed about five hundred pounds. Mothers in the wild—birds, mammals—no longer tolerated offspring when they reached a certain age—no more nursing, no more protecting them. They were on their own. So it was with farm animals, except that in this case, the mothers had no say in how or when the separation was done.

The day came. The semi-trucks arrived—one for the cows, one for the calves. The herd was driven by men on horseback into a small pasture next to the holding pens and the loading chute. From there the calves would be sent into one pen and the cows into an adjacent one. The gates were at ninety degrees to each other in a corner of the small pasture.

"You stand at this gate and let the calves into that pen,' Marvin yelled above all the mooing. "I'll be right over here at this gate letting the cows in through this one."

Sure. Sounds easy enough.

Well, those claves had spent all their lives near their mothers, and they weren't about to go somewhere without mom just because I wanted them to. This was worse, much worse, than getting them back into the pasture when they'd jumped the fence. I manned the corral gate, opening it when a calf came my way, closing it when the cow also tried to get through. It didn't work. Mother and calf were too quick for me. They both went through my gate, pushing it open and laughing at me as I fell down. I tried hard. I was nearly trampled many times.

"Close the gate quicker," Marvin yelled.

"I can't," I yelled back.

"Well, here." He motioned to me. "We'll change places. The mothers will go in this pen, and I'll take care of the calves."

I tried. "You damned bitch, get in here." She did, but I couldn't hold the gate closed, and her calf followed her, so we had me on the ground—again—and calves and cows in both pens. Give me a tractor to drive any day.

Marvin waved at one of the cowboys to come help. Suddenly, cows were going into one pen and calves into the other. I was sitting on top of a fence, clinging for my life, hoping one of those evil cows wouldn't jump up there on top of me.

Finally, cows and calves were separated and loaded into the cattle trucks. Marvin went along with Verne to help with the unloading. I went inside my house.

~ ~ ~

AN HOUR OR so later I heard a horse whinny. I wondered if someone got left behind, so I went out to the corrals—empty now—and discovered Verne's horse standing in the hot sun, reins dangling on the ground. I figured he was thirsty. I opened the gate that would allow him to get to the water trough and started back to the house. When he whinnied again, I looked back and saw he hadn't moved.

Hmmm. Now what do I do? I knew he could smell the water, and he wasn't tied up. What was the problem?

I went to him, rubbed his cheeks and neck, and talked to him.

"Come on," I said and started to walk away, hoping he would follow.

Nope. He whinnied and shook his head, bridle and reins flapping.

I walked back to him and stood toward the front of his head rubbing his soft nose and inhaling his horsey odor.

Suddenly, as if he'd made up his mind about something, he lifted his reins and draped them over my shoulder. Everything clicked into place. He was ground trained, which meant that when his reins were left dangling down on the ground, he wasn't supposed to move until somebody picked up the reins and led him.

So I did that. "You're a good, good horse," I told him as I led him—reins in my hand—to the water where he enjoyed a nice cool drink. I closed all the gates to that pen, lifted his reins onto the saddle so he could either pick a shady place to stand or go back to the trough for another drink.

That evening Verne came to get his good horse. His horse that was smarter than I was.

Cycles: We Plant Wheat Again – September 1983

WE PLANT THE wheat again in the warm September soil—just Marvin and me and the fresh clean dirt smell. I remember how afraid I was last year as I learned how to operate the machines that made possible the abundance of wheat that feeds us and the world. I feel an affinity for farmers long, long ago using pointed sticks to drill rows for seeds. In my mind's eye I see women or children reverently placing seeds in the rows, pleading with Mother Earth not to be angry with them for piercing her skin, asking Father Sky to send rain.

Methods and machinery are different now. Few farmers think of "their" fields as part of Mother Earth. They are thankful for the rain that waters their fields, but they don't have the same reverence for our soil, our earth.

I am of both worlds—split between the two viewpoints. The world is as it is, so I keep these thoughts to myself and help Marvin plant the seeds for next summer's crop.

Even in this new age of abundance, we are governed by the cycles of the seasons. The seeds we plant will sprout green and fresh. The sprouts will grow enough to look like lawn grass in the rows. Soon they will go dormant, sleeping under the soil and snow until they grow again in the spring and are ready for harvest in July.

Farmers are busy during the winter providing salt blocks, water, and twenty pounds of hay per day for each cow. Cows are bred (either naturally or artificially) in April or May so the calves will be born nine months later—rather like a human baby—in January or February. This is for the convenience of the markets. The calves will be at the right weight to be ready to be sold when the market is ready for them. That is, if they don't freeze to death in the winter blizzards. Marvin's cows dropped their calves in March's hopefully milder weather.

My parents once knew a couple who kept two milk cows. The man artificially inseminated his cows on the same day he inseminated his wife. Cows and wife produced offspring on the same day after nine months' gestation.

There are other cycles: school, religious or patriotic holidays, and, of course, the attendant greeting card cycles. In some way all of these human-made cycles are derived from the seasons. Long ago when children were a necessary part of the agricultural work force, they went to school during the winter and spring, and worked during the summer and fall doing whatever work they were capable of doing to make food for the coming winter. Now, summer usually means a time for holiday fun.

Early religions planned holy days at certain phases of the sun and moon—times significant for sowing, growing, and reaping. The winter solstice and Christmas were/are the harbinger of light returning to the earth. Easter occurs on the first Sunday after the first full moon after the spring equinox. It is the harbinger of the new growth of plants, animals, and a new religion.

Now we celebrate presidents' birthdays, independence days, memorial days, the ends of wars, famous battles—the list could go on and on. We honor these cycles on our calendars and with deluges of greeting cards that have nothing to do with the seasons of our natural world. They only clutter it with the detritus of confetti, streamers, fireworks, costumes, and many more such artificial things ad infinitum.

What happens to people when they do away with their natural cycles? I put away these thoughts and focus on the work of planting wheat.

At the Airport: Mommy Central – November 1983

THANKSGIVING DAY WAS fast approaching, and Virginia's daughter Anita, along with her husband Jim and twin daughters, Lori and Leigh, were coming from California to celebrate Thanksgiving at Mommy's house. They were scheduled to arrive two days before the holiday.

Marvin and I volunteered to pick them up at Stapleton airport in Denver. We had their flight information and the gate number where they were expected, so we moseyed down the concourse and waited. We were early, of course. Marvin was a stickler for being on time. To him, that meant being at least half an hour early. This time we were an hour early.

We waited.

The flight finally landed, but Anita and family were not among the passengers. We asked the gate attendant if she had any information about them. The only thing she knew was they weren't on the flight list for that plane or for any others on that airline.

We wandered the airport checking other airlines' gates but had no luck.

No one had cellphones at that time. We hadn't heard a page for us over the loudspeakers, so we did the only thing we could think of. We found a pay phone, and Marvin made a call.

"Hi, Mommy. We can't find them. They weren't on their flight."

"I know," she replied. "They called me just a few minutes ago. They got a better deal on a cheaper airline. Anita said they'd wait for you at the car rental place."

"Oh. Well, okay. It won't take us long to find where that is. Thanks, Mommy. See you in a couple of hours." I could hear Mommy laughing on the other end of the line as Marvin said goodbye. She had a great sense of humor. We were laughing, too.

We finally found them, and the story of Mommy as the central processing agent, keeping everyone straightened out, became another family story that was told and retold at every family gathering.

~ ~ ~

ANOTHER MOMMY STORY was about the time Marvin and I took her with us to the huge flea market on the north side of Denver. We rambled up and down the aisles looking over the merchandise and eating hot dogs. Pretty soon my legs and back were hurting, but Mommy was trudging along, seemingly unfazed by all the walking. He asked her once in a while if she was getting tired.

"No," she answered each time. "I'm fine." And she just kept marching right along.

Finally I gave up. "Well, I'm too tired to go any farther. I just hope I can make it back to the car."

"Yeah, I'm getting a little tired, too," Mommy admitted, although I was never sure whether she really was tired or whether she just didn't want to embarrass me. Even though she was in her eighties, she had way more stamina than I had.

~ ~ ~

WIDOWED IN 1971, after 50 years of marriage, Mommy was still the heart of the family. Everyone loved and respected her courage as she learned to live alone and manage her own affairs. With only an eighth-grade education, she had more of what Marvin and I called "walkin' around smarts" than anyone else we knew. Mommy spoke her mind, but never argued a point.

She was made of a sense of humor, and a whole bundle of love, smarts, courage, stamina, and good home cooking.

My Second Thanksgiving with the Family – November 1983

THE FAMILY WAS coming together again—nineteen people this year. When we arrived with Erica and Scott, Mommy was already with our host and hostess. Virginia and Eldred's daughter Anita, her husband and two grandchildren had spent the night with them after we brought them from the Denver airport. Their other daughter Marsha and her two boys had traveled the previous night from Fort Morgan. Sarah and Ron and their two sons arrived from Colorado Springs, then Walter and Ilene from Denver. Quite a crowd.

Having hosted the dinner the previous year and having gotten to know my new extended family throughout the previous year, this year I felt like I truly belonged.

The women who had spent the night before with Virginia and Eldred were creating the heavenly smell of roasting turkey, gravy, and homemade rolls. Others kept arriving with their own special dishes that had to be refrigerated or reheated. The women congregated in the kitchen while the men settled in the living room. Eldred kept everyone happy with his special eggnog. Soon the table was set and the feast was ready.

"Okay, everybody find a place to sit," Virginia directed over the hubbub.

"Here, Mommy," said Marvin. He pulled out the chair that would be the easiest for her to get into and out of.

The rest of us found places. Eldred said grace, and we all joined in with heartfelt *Amens*. Then we feasted on all that wonderful food.

As we began clearing the table I announced that since my only contribution to the meal had been a simple green bean concoction, I was going to be the dishwasher.

"Oh, you don't need to wash all those dishes," Virginia told me. "The dishwasher can hold most of the dishes, and we can run two loads."

"Okay," I said. "Then I'll do the pots and pans." Some of the other women had already been emptying them and storing the leftovers for later, so I rolled up my sleeves, put on an apron, ran a sink full of soapy water and started in on my new job. From then on, that was my job at the family dinners—except for the ones where I was the hostess. It suited me. I was in the kitchen enjoying the company of the other women, and the job didn't require a lot of thinking. Plus, I knew my cooking skills didn't measure up to those of the other women. So, to me this was the easiest way I could be helpful.

Others grabbed dishtowels and began to dry the pots and pans and put them away. We had an efficient assembly line going, so it didn't take long to get the kitchen tidied up.

When we joined the men in the living room the conversation was, as usual, enquiries about distant relatives and family stories.

That year I had a story to tell—the one about the ground-tied horse teaching me how I had to release him so he could get a drink of water. Everyone laughed about that good horse.

Eldred said, "Marvin, I think I saw that cutting horse you used to have. She was in a pasture over by Fort Morgan—must be pretty old by now."

"Yeah. I sold her sometime around '78 or '79, about when I sold my cows. She sure was a good cutting horse. When I first got her, I had a helluva time getting her to do what I wanted, but after a while I found out that if I just pointed her toward the cow I wanted to cut out of the herd, all I had to do was drop the reins and hold onto the saddle horn. She'd do the rest of the job."

He paused a moment and a slow smile spread across his face. "I was checking the cows one day when I found a neighbor's bull in the pasture with my two hundred head of heifers. I showed my horse the bull that I wanted her to cut out of the herd. That horse got right over the back of that bull, and if he slowed down or tried to go in another direction, she'd nip him right hard on the back. Away we went running almost a mile as fast as we could go."

Marvin's smile widened even further. "He never got in my pasture again."

Time Becomes Timeless – Spring 1984

AFTER TWO YEARS of being a farm wife, two years of learning new skills, two years of living the seasonal cycles of farming, things seemed to change. Or maybe it was just that I finally settled comfortably into this farm life.

One morning we woke to the sound of a gazillion frogs singing like one voice. Spring had arrived. The green shoots of wheat were breaking through the dirt and getting taller every day. The sun warmed our backs as Marvin and I fixed fences in anticipation of the cattle that would arrive as soon as there was enough grass for them.

To my relief, the cows that came to our pasture in April did not include the bitch cow that had been so ornery the past two summers, jumping fences and leading the rest of the herd into the neighbor's fields.

The new leader calmly led the cows out of the stock trailer in the west pasture, then over the fence (*Oh no!*) to munch on new shoots of grass and weeds along the fence line and in the barrow ditch. When they were full, they slowly walked across the road, into our yard, stopped beside the house where they chewed their cuds and stared at me through the dining room window. They seemed to be inspecting my housekeeping—or maybe they were just curious about why anybody would stay in a box when they could easily be outside in the fresh air. When they got tired of looking at me, they proceeded to the gate that held them back from the east pasture. They mooed until I open the gate for them.

From then on, they had me trained.

Marvin just laughed.

Cindy, My Samoyed – Spring 1984

ON A BEAUTIFUL spring morning Cindy died suddenly of an apparent heart attack at age ten. We wrapped her body in a clean white sheet and buried her under a large elm tree.

That evening we talked about the various things she had done in her life. Erica told about long ago when we lived in Steamboat Springs. Cindy's sled dog heritage came alive when we got a harness for her. When we cut a Christmas tree in the forest, she pulled it to the pickup with great enthusiasm.

One of her greatest joys was helping us pull our heavy toboggan up the hill beside our house and then racing beside it while we rode down to where she went into a frenzy of anticipation waiting for us to hook her harness to the toboggan again.

Then I remembered the time Puddy Tat, Erica's cat, had kittens. When Puddy Tat took a break from the arduous task of motherhood, Cindy curled herself around the kittens to keep them clean and warm.

We talked about how intent she was when she tried to find whatever was making those rustling noises in the old motor in the round-top.

We missed her.

Hector

SCOTT BROUGHT HOME a dirty, shaggy dog with him one day and announced that the dog's name was Hector. He'd obviously been an outdoor dog. "Well," I said, "he'd better not pee in the house." But it turned out that Hector was a perfect gentleman.

He was about two feet tall with a medium build. His coat was mostly black with brown, white, and tan areas. As I gently brushed the burrs and matted hair out of the multicolored coat, I noticed that only the tips of the black hair patches were colored, while the inner part was white. I treated him to a bit of cod liver oil every day, and soon his coat was soft and glossy. Sometimes I forgot to give him his cod liver oil. As a reminder to me, Hector would stand patiently in front of the refrigerator with his nose pressed against the door until I remembered to get the oil for him.

Someone told us that Hector was part Bernese Mountain dog. I did some research and found that he did resemble that breed both in character and physically (although he wasn't quite as big as they usually grew). He was calm, friendly, protective, and not given to excessive barking. We never found out from what other breed he might have come.

He accompanied me on walks along the country roads. As I walked, he explored a two-hundred-foot circle around me. I never knew he was guarding me until the day I stopped suddenly and sat down on the road to get a rock out of my shoe. Within seconds he was there beside me sniffing, enquiring. He stayed rooted until I retied my laces and resumed my walk.

Dammit! – Fall 1984

MARVIN HAD TOLD me several times that his father liked to keep up with the times. They'd gotten electricity and a telephone line to the farmhouse before many of their neighbors. Later, when they moved into town, Marvin's dad and mom bought a new-fangled contraption called a television. So, following in the family tradition, Marvin came to me one day and said, "Honey, I think we should get a computer."

About that same time one of our relatives invested in a new computer company called Westron Corporation. We visited the company headquarters in Denver, met the owner and a salesman, and decided to invest and buy one of their computers.

Our new computer was delivered by Parcel Post about a month later. The package was too big for our rural mailbox, so the postman left the package sitting on the ground beside the post. I was home when he left it, but I didn't know it was there. Luckily, the rural farm community was an honest one, so even if I'd known it was there, I wouldn't have worried.

When Marvin came home, he burst into the house. "Look, Honey! Our computer is here!" We unpacked it and followed the diagrams to set it up and turn it on. Our computer flickered a bit, then showed a black and white screen with the characters *DOS_* in the upper left corner.

Marvin sat in front of our new gadget and pressed some keys. We both stared at the screen that had some lines and numbers. Marvin got up and said, "Honey, you sit here. You probably know more about this than I do."

We traded places. I pressed some keys and got the same results Marvin had gotten.

I knew I was in deep doodoo. "I have no idea what to do."

The next day I went to the library and asked the librarian if she knew what *DOS_* meant. She didn't. I went back home and made a phone call.

"Westron Corporation," said a nice voice. "How may I help you?"

"This is Diana Alishouse," I told her. "We received our computer yesterday but don't know how it works or what to do with it."

"Oh." She sounded confused. "Isn't the *DOS_* handbook in the package?"

"No."

"I'm so sorry. I'll get one in the mail to you today."

"Will it tell us how to work on our computer?"

"Yes, ma'am. It has everything you need to know."

Two weeks later we received the handbook. We had no idea what all the jargon meant.

I enrolled in a computer class at a nearby junior college. S-l-o-w-l-y, v-e-e-r-y s-l-o-w-l-y, I began to make a bit of sense out of that machine. It was a lot harder and a lot less fun than the tractor, combine, and trucks. Eventually we purchased a WYSIWYG (What You See Is What You Get) computer, and I didn't have to put up with DOS any longer.

One night Marvin was sitting in his chair watching TV while I was in the office creating a spreadsheet showing our budget for the next year. I was elated—no more hand entries into the columns on a piece of paper, no more punching numbers into my old calculator then checking the numbers on the roll of adding machine tape!

I completed the budget, grabbed the printout, and bounced into the living room.

"Look what I did," I crowed as I began explaining all the rows and columns. "According to this we'll be able to pay all expenses—business and personal—and still have this much left over."

He studied the spreadsheet for a while then picked up a small pad of paper, the kind politicians hand out during election years, the kind that fits in a man's shirt pocket. On the pad were a few numbers. He pointed to the one at the bottom. It was within a thousand dollars of the figure I'd come up with.

Dammit! After all that work!

The Hershey Bar – August 1984

EVERY YEAR THE Agricultural Service Center (ASC), part of the U.S. Department of Agriculture Farm Service Agency, determined the number of acres of wheat they allowed us to plant. If we had a field left over, we planted it with hershey, commonly known as millet and used for birdseed. The grain elevator in Akron also ran a birdseed packaging business.

We stored our hershey in a seldom-used bin and didn't think much about it until we began hauling it to the birdseed plant. Before we emptied the bin, by chance my parents were coming to visit with us for a few days.

One evening a couple of weeks before they arrived, as I was cooking supper, Marvin came in with a wicked grin on his face.

"Okay," I said. "What are you thinking up this time?"

"Well, your mother likes chocolate candy, doesn't she?"

"Yeah."

"Why don't we make her a hershey bar?"

"Huh?"

"You know—hershey?"

It took me a minute to figure out what he was talking about. "Oh!" I finally said. "A *hershey* bar."

"Yep." His grin widened.

I thought about it. "I don't know," I said tentatively. "You know how prickly she can be when she's not in charge."

We threw ideas around until I came up with something that I thought might work. "Honey, if *I* do it, she'll get mad. If *you* do it, she'll see it as the joke we want it to be. What do you think?"

"You're right. Remember when I had her believing I owned an airplane? And the time at their house when I told her I only liked two kinds of pie. She kind of wilted until I said *hot and cold.*"

"Okay," I said. "That'll work. I'll act really surprised, so she won't think I was in on it." I hated that kind of deception, but my mother's temper was no fun to put up with. "We'll need to buy one of the regular Hershey bars next time we go into town so we'll have the wrapper."

How were we going to get the hershey into it, though? Neither one of us of thought it would work if we melted the whole Hershey bar. We'd never get it back into the right shape. And it had to be that distinctive oblong shape.

We pondered the idea for several days and finally got Erica and Scott in on the surprise we were planning for their grandma and grandpa. We decided to soften a Hershey Bar just enough so we could press the hershey seeds into the bottom of it. That way we wouldn't mess up the distinctive markings on the top of the bar.

We bought enough Hershey bars for experimentation. After several prototypes, which we had to throw away—or eat—we came up with the perfect Hershey Bar for Grandma. It looked like an unopened store-bought candy bar. We'd softened the chocolate enough so that it sort of settled around the millet. This way, the individual seeds didn't show.

The afternoon arrived, we talked about our millet crop, showed them the bin where it was stored and explained that in Colorado it was called hershey.

"It looks like birdseed," was all Mama said.

Marvin explained that yes, it was birdseed, and that millet was also cooked and eaten as a grain in Europe and other parts of the world.

After lunch, Marvin handed out candy bars to everyone. When Mama took a bite out of hers she choked a little bit, made a face, and demanded, "What **is** this?"

We all began laughing and I could see her starting to get riled up until Marvin stepped in and took over. He took her candy bar, took a big bite of it himself, and said, "It's my special kind of hershey bar."

"Oh, you silly man," she said with a smile.

I couldn't let Marvin have all the fun, though. I had a nice dinner for all of us. When I'd finished eating, I put my plate on the floor for Hector to lick clean. Then I picked it up and put it back into the cupboard. My mother gasped. "Diana Jean, just what do you think you're doing? I raised you better than that!"

I just looked at her and grinned.

But then I pulled the plate back out and put it in the sink.

Brockle and Broccoli – September 1984

THERE WERE FIVE of those babies—three weighing three hundred pounds each and two weighing only two hundred and fifty pounds each. They weren't fully weaned yet. Marvin nodded his head, and the auctioneer cried, "Sold! What's your number sir?" Marvin flashed his card at the auctioneer. We went to the auction office, paid for the calves, and then pulled the cattle trailer around to the loading chute. The calves weren't happy.

"Poor babies," I said. They'd been separated from their mothers, trucked with a lot of other calves to the sale barn, hazed through the arena, then run through a chute into our trailer. They must have been scared to death, thirsty, and probably hungry.

We stopped in town to get milk replacement, and then headed home where we backed the trailer up to the loading chute. We let the calves out into the small holding pen. From the pen they moved into a stall in the barn where they immediately bunched up for the only kind of protection they could imagine.

We'd bought the calves for Erica and Scott to take care of through the winter and sell next spring. They'd learn something and have money to buy a car or pay for college tuition. When the school bus stopped in our yard that Friday afternoon, Erica and Scott immediately heard the calves bawling, and ran to the barn to see what was happening.

Marvin stood in the stall with the young calves and watched them, letting them get used to his presence, touching them with his strong hands, firmly and gently, little finger curved in tight against his ring finger. He was strong, but wary. He knew what damage even a small calf could do to a man.

How can such strong hands be so gentle when he touches me, I wondered. I was in the alleyway looking through the gaps between the boards at the calves and at Marvin.

The calves were calming down, but as soon as Erica and Scott burst through the barn door and began yammering, the calves started bawling and bunching together again.

"Come on, kids," Marvin said. "We need to let them settle down. Let's go to the house, and I'll explain about the calves."

As we walked toward the house, Marvin talked. "You'll take turns every morning getting up early, cleaning the stall, feeding, and getting to know the habits of each calf. In the winter it'll be tough to get up so early. You may have to shovel your way to the barn. If the snow is too deep, I'll plow a path for you."

"Yes!" exclaimed Scott, the farm boy. "Oh, geez," said Erica, the city girl.

"Go change your clothes so you can feed your calves," Marvin directed.

"Now?" they both asked.

"Yes," I said. "Now. They need milk."

Their first lesson began as Marvin got the milk replacement and bottles. I got out the measuring cups and helped the kids with mixing together the right amount of powder and lukewarm water. When the bottles were filled, we all went to the barn.

"Stick one hand between the boards palm side up with your first two fingers out, like this." Marvin showed them what to do. The nearest calf came over and began sucking greedily at his two fingers. The kids and I tried it too.

"Careful," Marvin warned. "These kids are strong. Don't get your arm between the board where a calf might lean against it. You could wind up with a broken arm."

Both kids pulled their hands back a bit farther.

"Now, hold the bottle almost upside down where the calf can get to it."

The calves were hungry after their recent ordeal, so they quickly guzzled the milk. I hoped calves wouldn't throw up the way human babies did when they gorged too much.

"You have to keep the stall clean. The manure shovel is right here." Marvin pointed. "Put the manure in the manure pile in the big corral. When the pile gets big, I'll move it with the front-loader. Fill the tank with water. Put some hay in the manger so they'll get used to eating it. When you leave, make sure the gates and the door are closed."

That's a lot of information to keep straight, I thought as we started toward the house.

"Did you give them water and hay, and did you close the gate and the door?" Marvin asked.

Without a word they turned around and went back to the barn. Eventually they came to the house and announced that they'd decided they'd get up together and do the chores together for the next two days.

"Might as well start your homework now," I told the kids. "That way you'll have time over the weekend to learn about the calves and get used to taking care of them."

The next morning I woke earlier than usual. Both kids were gone. *Either they've run away or they're in the barn,* I thought. *This'll be good for both of them.* I went back to bed.

At breakfast Erica declared that she thought we should give the calves names, so we'd know which one we were talking about.

"That's fine," said Marvin. "Just don't forget that they're not pets. They'll be going to the sale barn next spring. Think about the money."

The naming began with Erica. "I think the little one with all the white should be named Bright." Everyone agreed.

"What about the little brockle-faced one?" asked Marvin.

"What's a brockle face?"

Erica wasn't the only one wondering that.

"It means his face is unevenly colored," Marvin explained.

"One of the big ones is brockled, too," Scott pointed out.

"Yeah, but he isn't as cute as the little one," I inserted. "Besides, we can't have two calves with the same name."

Erica had the solution. "How about we call the big one Brockle and the little one Broccoli?"

Eventually we got the others named. Brownie, because he was—duh—brown; Bright for the one with all the white on his back; and George because we couldn't think of anything else.

~ ~ ~

WHILE THE KIDS were in school and the weather was still cold, Marvin told me it was time to dock the young bulls. "I talked to Lewis"—a longtime friend—"the other day and he can come help us tomorrow."

I noticed the *us* in that sentence.

"Don't worry," he said. "Louis and I will do most of it. I just thought it would be interesting for you to learn how it's done."

"Oh," I said.

At the appointed time, donned in my coveralls and work gloves, I followed Marvin and Louis to the corral by the barn.

Louis grabbed one of the bulls and put it on the ground on its side. Marvin jammed one knee into the hollow in front of the bull's back leg. With his left hand he grabbed the lower foreleg just above the hoof, cramped it so the bull couldn't kick, and grabbed the bull's ear and held it over the bull's eye. Within seconds the bull was rendered immobile.

Louis cut the end of the bull's sac off and slipped the testicles out. Marvin released the former bull—now technically a steer—and I wondered which end of the next bull I'd be working on. Answer, the end with the blood.

Louis laid down a bull. Marvin stood close behind me and coached. My knee went into the hollow behind the back leg. My left hand grabbed the forefoot. My right hand covered the bull's eye with his ear. My legs and arms were cramping with the effort. Louis did his work. The calf bawled. Marvin said, "Okay, let go of everything at once and jump back out of the way."

"I can't," I yelled.

"Why not?"

"I don't think I can move."

"Yes, you can."

"No."

"Yes."

"Shit," I yelled and forced my leg muscles to let go and jump back.

It was a good thing I managed it. That steer was *not* happy.

~ ~ ~

ONE DAY IN the spring when the snow had melted off and Scott and Erica were at school, Marvin said, "It's time to take the cows to the sale barn."

"You mean without telling the kids? They won't get to say goodbye. Won't that be hard for them to take?"

"Maybe, but we can't wait till they have a school holiday. We have other things to do. Besides, we told them not to get attached to them."

Dammit. *I* was attached to them. I hadn't learned my lesson.

They were bigger now. Much bigger. And dirty with mud and manure. That helped my feelings a little bit as I petted them for the last time, helped with the loading, and got into the pickup.

When the kids came home from school, Marvin handed each of them a check. None of us cried. That's the way farming is.

The Prize-Winning Recipe – March 1985

ONE EVENING I found a casserole recipe in a farm magazine. The article praised the recipe as having won first prize in a county fair somewhere or other, so I cut it out and took it with me to the grocery store the next week. One of the ingredients seemed strange for a beef casserole—it was something I didn't keep on hand—but I liked to try new things occasionally, so I added it to my cart.

When I got around to try the new recipe, I measured the ingredients carefully because of that unusual one. The aroma of the baking casserole was enticing. The four of us sat down to supper and passed the casserole, green beans, salad, and bread around the table. Scott was the first one to take a bite. He got a funny look on his face as he put down his fork, took a big drink of water, and started buttering his bread. By the time he'd finished, Marvin and Erica both had that same look.

"What's wrong?" I asked.

They all spoke at the same time. "Taste it."

I did. It had an awful sweetish taste with a tang of something that would have been unidentifiable except that I knew what that weird ingredient had been. Yuck!

I warmed up some chili that was left over from the previous night. By the time the chili was warm, the casserole was cool, so I set it on the floor for Hector. He came running when he heard the sound of me setting down that baking dish.

He ran to it, stopped, sniffed. Then he turned to me with a baleful look and walked away.

The unusual ingredient? Ginger snaps! I never did figure out how the casserole could smell so good but taste so horrible. Maybe it was an editorial oversight. For sure it wouldn't have won first prize tasting like this!

I threw away the casserole AND the recipe.

Un Bel Di – Spring 1985

IN MAY, ERICA graduated from Akron High School along with many friends. She spent that summer as usual with her father, a silversmith who lived in Tucson, where she found work at a Wendy's Restaurant. Tamra finished college at the University of Nebraska at Kearney and moved to Los Angeles. In September Erica returned and began as an English major at the University of Northern Colorado. Marvin and I just kept farming.

One day a neighbor needed help, so Marvin got me started tilling the field just south of the house, then got in his pickup and went to help the neighbor. This was the first time we'd worked the ground that spring. The soil was easy to turn, and I was happy to be in our big articulated 4800 Massey Ferguson tractor preparing the lovely soil for next year's crop.

I was driving the tractor south next to the road and had gone about halfway down that side of the field when the implement sank into the ground. I got out and surveyed the situation. The sweeps were buried all the way up to the shanks to where they were bolted to the implement. I got back in and worked the hydraulic levers to lift everything out of the ground.

Nothing moved.

I knew better than to try to "rock" the tractor back and forth. That might work for a car or a pickup, but not for a tractor with an implement behind.

"Shit. If I try to force the hydraulics, I might break the implement." I don't know who I was talking to, but I had to vent somehow.

I knew exactly what Marvin would say when he got home. *Wellwhudjadothatfor?*

The only thing I could think of to do was walk back home and plan a wonderfully delicious meal for that evening. As soon as I turned the tractor off, though, I heard his pickup, turned, and confirmed that the dust cloud coming down the road was his.

Marvin, who was returning to get a tool he needed, came boiling to a stop, jumped out of the pickup and across the ditch and said *Wellwhudjadothatfor?* Whereupon my brain turned to mush trying to find the words to explain what I'd done. He turned the tractor on, worked the hydraulic levers, and gently pulled the implement out of the ground. I had no idea what he'd done that I hadn't thought to do.

"Oh," he tossed off casually, "I forgot to tell you about that soft spot. You can keep going now." He threw me a kiss and was gone.

I climbed back into the tractor and finished making the beautiful furrows on that side of the field and then turned left heading east. Everything was peachy until about halfway down the field when I noticed I was dragging some barbed wire and a fence post.

I lifted the implement, throttled the tractor down, climbed out of the cab, and went to see what I could do. The barbed wire was wrapped only once around the outside sweep on the implement and was barely attached to the fence post by a very loose staple. I put on my gloves and worked the barbed wire off the sweep, then got a big screwdriver from the tractor to pull the staple out of the rotten wood. I moved the whole mess into the next field and made a note to tell Marvin about it so we wouldn't pick it up when we got around to doing that field. That was probably how I'd snagged it this time. Somebody threw it over the fence and then forgot about it. I wondered how many times that particular rotten post would make the trip between fields.

The rest of the day's work had an easy rhythm. The tractor purred with its deep bass voice. I sang along with Puccini's aria, *Un Bel Di,* from his opera *Madam Butterfly*. And countless birds swooped to the turned earth looking for worms. Lovely.

Winding Down – Fall 1985

THAT AUTUMN WE were busy with all the ordinary chores of farming—sowing seeds for next year's crop, fixing fences, tilling fields, chasing cows back into the pasture. In our free time we visited with friends at The Hearty Rancher Café or went to see how Mommy was doing. She usually had something deliciously fattening for us to eat. Scott was a sophomore in high school and played on the basketball team, so we went to all the home games and a few of the away games.

One night Marvin and I could not get to sleep. The light coming in our bedroom window at the head of the bed was strange. It wasn't moonlight or a fire, and it kind of flickered. Finally we got up and knelt, leaning against the headboard, to see what was happening. What we saw was cloud-to-cloud lightning on the distant horizon. What a display. We couldn't hear any thunder, but stayed up late to enjoy the fantastic lightshow.

The next morning we were tired, but we had work to do. Two scruffy twenty-foot elm trees growing close to the concrete pad in front of the shop doors were getting big enough that roots could start heaving the concrete. Marvin had dug trenches around them and watered them for several days to loosen the soil. Now the ground was soft enough.

He came in the house where I was cooking.

"Can you come help me get those elms out of the way?" he asked.

I turned off the stovetop.

"I've got the ropes around them. I just want you to pull them out with the tractor."

Ooooh! I thought. *This'll be way more fun than cooking.*

I grabbed my trusty work gloves and climbed into the tractor.

Marvin coached me. "Put it in low gear, and take it slow. We're pulling out the one farthest from the shop first."

I did as he said and tapped the throttle. Not much happened, so I nudged the throttle up a little more and felt the tree move. Gently, I kept on that tree until it eased out of the ground.

"Now drag it into that hole in the pasture where we used to make silage. The pasture gate is already open. I'll come along in the pickup and help you get the ropes off the tree. Then we can come get the other one out."

It sounded like we'd be busy for quite a while. *That's okay. I can defrost some of the stew I made last week.* I sure was glad we had a big freezer so I could play on the tractor!

~ ~ ~

WE HAD MANY elms trees around the house and down the hill to the creek. The early settlers, Marvin's parents, had planted the fast-growing elms around the homestead to shield the house, barns, and corrals from the bitter winter winds. Now those big trees were getting toward the end of their lives, and I knew we'd eventually have to cut them down. I thought happily of days in the tractor pulling trees out of the dirt.

But other chores intervened, and we never did get around to taking out those other trees. Someone else would do it after we were gone.

Drinks At the Airport – December 1985

EIGHT OF US were waiting to greet our daughter Tamra. She'd moved to California last spring after graduating from college. Besides Marvin and me, there were two children, two grandchildren, and a couple of their friends. We ranged in age from three years to forty-something.

"I'm thirsty," said one child.

"Me, too," the rest of them clamored.

My husband in his calm manner, offered to get everyone a soft drink and was bombarded with orders—all of them of a different size and brand. He listened to them carefully, then asked me to come help him carry the drinks while the kids stayed where they were. "There'll be less confusion that way," he said.

I struggled to remember what each person wanted, thinking *This is going to be a mess. What if we get it wrong?*

We got to the head of the line, and my husband ordered eight medium Pepsis to go. I shut my mouth on the list I'd been trying to help him remember.

When we returned to the clutch of kids, they all crowded around us.

"That's one's mine."

"No, I wanted a large one."

"I get the Dr. Pepper. Where is it?"

Noisily they searched for their drinks.

Then, in a sudden silence of realization, they stared at their dad, their grandpa. Each one picked up a medium Pepsi, thanked him, and we all proceeded to enjoy our drinks, finishing just in time to make it to the gate to see Tamra disembark.

The Bridge Inspector – January 1986

SINCE THAT FIRST year, 1983, when I helped Marvin haul wheat to the elevator, we'd done it together every year. This year was no exception. The process went smoothly as we took several truckloads to town. After our final trip for the day, we were coming home empty. When we got to the bridge across the intermittent creek that ran beside the farmstead we found a pickup parked in the middle of the road and a man waving his arms to flag us down. Marvin stopped. We got out of the cab. The man introduced himself as the bridge inspector.

"I can't let you go this way. The whole structure is full of dry rot, and I've condemned it. It could collapse at any time."

"Can't I go over it one more time just to get home? This was my final load for the day and I'm empty." Marvin pointed ahead. "That's my house right there."

The inspector shuffled his feet as he thought. "Well," he finally said, "I guess … what's your empty weight?"

"Twenty-thousand-one-hundred-eighty pounds," I said. They both gave me startled looks. "I looked it up just a few days ago before we started hauling."

The inspector was still looking at me funny. "I'm a bookkeeper," I told him. "I was working on a list of machinery for our CPA, and I needed the empty weight."

"Well," he finally said, "I guess you can go over it just this once. But from now on you'll have to go around."

We nodded, thanked him, and drove slowly over the bridge, into our driveway, and into the shop building.

The next day … and the next … we drove fully loaded over the bridge.

It didn't collapse.

The Dove Hunters – October 1986

ONE DAY WE came home from town to find an army of dove hunters hunkered down in the barrow ditch with guns pointed outward toward us as we turned from Baseline Road onto Road JJ. We also noticed that they'd opened the gate to one of our pastures and parked their vehicles there.

Marvin, in his usual placid but determined manner, got out of our pickup. "Did you get permission to hunt here?"

"Yessir," replied one of the hunters. "We asked the man up there," and he pointed at our house.

"No, you didn't. I'm the owner of this land and that house, and you're breaking the law because you didn't get my permission. You're also breaking the law for shooting too close to a house."

At that point two men with hunting dogs appeared behind the hunters, and a bevy of doves flew up in panic. Even though they escaped right over the hunters, there was not a single shot. When the flurry of birds died down, Marvin said, "And I don't allow hunting dogs on my land. They give hunters an unfair advantage. It's time for you to leave … don't forget to close the gate."

I was scared to death. We had no protection except Marvin's formidable and confident demeanor, which turned out to be the only thing we needed. The men gathered their gear, got into the vehicles they'd parked on our land, and left ... closing the gate behind them.

Burning a Bridge – Spring 1987

WHEAT WAS GROWING, fences had been fixed, cows were in the pasture, the windmill was working. And Bill, the county road supervisor showed up early one morning for coffee.

"Well, he said, "I guess you already know we're going to be starting on a new bridge pretty soon."

"Yeah," Marvin said. "I figured that when we saw the survey guys."

Bill turned to me. "Don't worry. We'll doze a good bypass on the west side of the bridge so you can get to town for groceries."

The next day we woke to the sound of big machinery—dump trucks hauling gravel and sand, and a bulldozer to push it around. A few days later we had a bypass. A few days after that the road crew showed up and knocked down the bridge supports with the bulldozer. That old bridge collapsed immediately and completely into a pile in the creek bed. I guess the inspector had been right about the dry rot.

Bill yelled at me, "Diana, come here! You get to set it on fire."

The crew doused the wood with diesel fuel, and I tossed a burning piece of wood onto the remains of the bridge. It took a while to catch fire, but when it did, it burned a long time.

Building the new steel bridge took most of that spring, but I was okay. After all, I had my very own bypass so I could get to town. And I had a new take on the old saying about *burning your bridges.*

More Winding Down – 1987 through 1989

ONE DAY DURING the late summer of 1987 Marvin came into the house and said, "I need to be around more people." We'd been talking a lot about the future. We'd even bought a house in town. Scott was about to begin his senior year in high school and would play on the varsity basketball team, so it made sense for us to live in town where he was close to the school.

Our dog Hector went with us of course and explored his new neighborhood. Soon after we moved there, he brought home an ice cream bucket full of dogfood. A few weeks later he proudly brought us a cast iron skillet filled with the remains of hamburger goulash. His "gifts" continued—eventually including a large glass Pyrex baking dish. How he managed to carry that monster home we never knew. I placed his purloined gifts in a row at the curb of our house with a sign telling neighbors to pick up their dishes, skillets, pots, and pans. Some of them disappeared. We never knew whether the owners found their property or if Hector took them to somebody else's house. No one took the Pyrex dish, so I finally claimed it. Now, more than thirty years later, I still have it. And it works just fine.

One night that fall after Marvin and I went to bed, Hector was restless, pacing back and forth refusing to go to sleep. Finally, I got out of bed said, "Okay. Show me what's wrong." He immediately started down the hallway to the living room, then through the kitchen, often glancing back at me to be sure I was following. When we got to the top of the stairs leading to the basement, Hector sat and stared. I figured out what was wrong—contrary to my usual custom I'd left the basement light on and Hector knew that wasn't right. I went down the stairs and turned out the light. As I climbed the stairs, I thanked Hector for alerting me to something that was wrong. I'd swear his gentle *whuff* meant *you're welcome.* Then we both headed back to bed and a good night's sleep.

He continued his self-appointed job of keeping an eye on the house and family. He was a calm presence in our lives for many years. As he got older, though, all he wanted to do was lie on a mat by the front door.

When he died, we buried him on the farm under the elm next to Cindy, my loving Samoyed.

Along about then, with excellent timing for us, the U.S. government offered a conservation Reserve Program (CRP). We were able to put our crop land into the program and receive a cash payment. There was a stipulation that we had to seed and grow native Prairie short-grass on the CPR land.

The only land we had for a crop then was the school section that we rented from the State of Colorado. The rental money went into the state education budget.

A section of land is 640 acres (one mile by one mile), so each year we worked only 320 acres of wheat and that left 320 acres of summer fallow. We still tilled the soil in the spring and summer and harvested the wheat in July. I didn't get to drive the tractor much, but I rode with Marvin sometimes. Also, we still had to maintain fences, the windmills, and the buildings.

A Good Corner Post – 1989

AS WE ATE our supper Marvin asked if I had anything to do the next day. "A corner post in the big pasture needs to be replaced," he told me. "It won't take too long."

Right, I thought. So many jobs that *wouldn't take too long* ended up being half- or full-day affairs.

"In the morning we'll get some barbed wire, three good solid railroad ties, a couple of round fence posts, fence staples, and two short lengths of wood for tightening the barbed wire. I'll go ahead tonight and get the shovel, post hole digger, hammer, and fencing tool from the shop."

Right, I thought again. *Won't take long at all.*

I went to bed and thought about the bookkeeping waiting for me. I needed to get it done, but I knew a day of manual work with Marvin would be a lot more fun.

We headed to the farm.

"How are we going to get all the existing stuff out of the way?" I asked.

"That's easy," he said. "We get the little tractor and pull all the junk out of the dirt and haul it away."

"Oh." *I get to drive the tractor!*

"Now we dig three holes for the railroad ties. The sturdiest tie will be the corner post."

I followed his directions as we put the other two into the ground ninety degrees from the corner post. That way we had a right triangle. I mentally labeled the posts A, B, and C, with B as the corner post.

Then we put a round fence post laterally from the top of corner post (B) to the top of one of the secondary posts (A) and tacked it into position. We tacked the other round fence post between B and C. The whole thing looked completely unstable to me.

But Marvin knew what he was doing. He turned to the roll of barbed wire, found the end of it, and made several loops around the top of Post A. Then he ran the barbed wire to the bottom of the corner post (B), then back to Post A.

"See," he said. "Now I can put a stick between the two strands of barbed wire and turn the stick—rotate it so it'll tighten the barbed wire and apply pressure between the corner post and this one." He patted Post A as if it were a puppy.

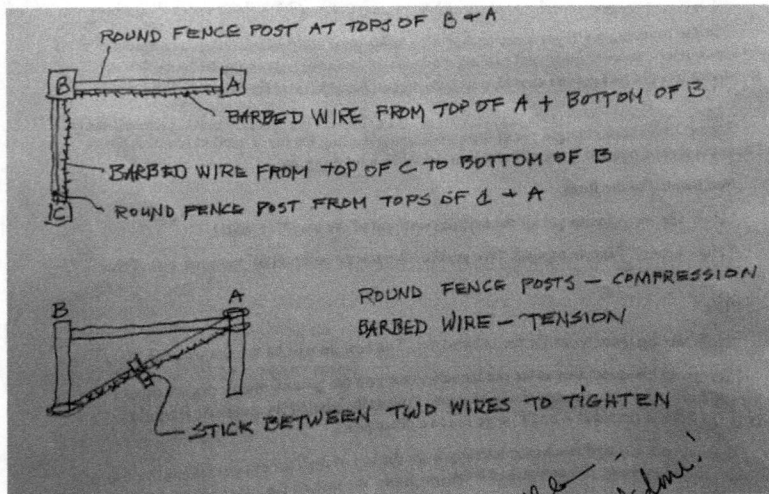

Aha, I thought. *Now there's a triangle that will keep things stable—one member is stretched and the other is compressed.* It reminded me somewhat of how a good stable family works. There's usually a corner post person, attached to the others in several different ways—sometimes the two are close together, sometimes they seem to strain against each other. But the corner post stays stable through it all. Building a good fence corner was a lot like building the character of a good family.

I'd been meditating too long. "Now we do the same thing between the corner post and that one?" I suggested.

"That's right. Then everything will be stable once the barbed wire is tightened."

We loaded our tools and the extra barbed wire into the pickup and headed for home. On the way I asked him how he figured out how to do that.

He pondered a while. "I don't know," he finally said. "I guess I just picked it up from my dad and other farmers."

So, sometime, probably a very long time ago, some enterprising person discovered this way of stabilizing a corner post, passed it down to the children, and the idea spread.

Whoever that person was, I sure was grateful.

~ ~ ~

LATER THAT YEAR, when our CRP contract expired, we rented the farm to Brett, a young man who wanted to be a farmer and hoped to buy our farm within a few years.

We began hauling the wheat we had stored, and by 2004 had taken all of it to the grain elevator in town. The harvest spreadsheet on which I'd kept track of all the wheat we'd stored in our bins and round-top was within one thousand bushels of the elevator's tally. That may sound like a lot, but it's really a small discrepancy when you consider that our blue truck would hold 650 bushels. All those years of wheat-growing and selling, and I was off by only one and a half truck loads.

We sold the farm to Brett in increments from over the next five years.

I was no longer a farm wife.
I still miss the tractor.

Everything is Different – May 2018

IT ISN'T THE same. Most of our fields—the ones that used to be ours—are covered with wheat or corn, and none of them are allowed to rest and rejuvenate themselves by lying fallow through the summer. The rest have giant machines with huge booms spraying the fields to kill weeds where corn or sunflowers grew last year. When will they be seeded for another crop? What will it be?

The spring in the west pasture has dried up. The dam that held back sudden flooding from summer rains is gone.

One pickup sits in the drive, but no one is home. Our lawn that snuggled around the house is gone. The chicken house is gone. The shop and round-top have been painted with glaring silver paint that hurts my eyes.

The big elm trees I thought we'd be cutting down are gone, felled by someone else. I suppose the bones of Cindy and Hector were torn up like the trees.

The only sign of our previous presence is the remaining twenty-foot-long row of irises that marked the edge of my garden.

And I still miss the tractor.

~ ~ ~

Acknowledgements

My thanks, first and foremost, to my husband Marvin, who supported me in so many ways throughout my farm wife journey, in sickness and in health, for better or worse. Through all the months (years) of teaching me about farming, Marvin never got angry about my mistakes. The worst he ever said was "Well, whudja do that for?" From him I learned patience and how to rein in the volatile temper I'd learned in early life from my mother. I cradle that knowledge, for I recognize how much being a farm wife—being Marvin's farm wife—changed my life for the better.

Many thanks, too, to my sister, Fran Stewart, for encouraging me to write these stories and then for reading them, loving them, and editing them.

And last, to the conscientious members of my writing group, who offered so many helpful suggestions as I slogged my way through this process. I appreciate each and every one of you.

About the Author

Diana Alishouse, raised in an Air Force family, learned early to adapt to the frequent moves and to use her mathematical intelligence and her artistic abilities to solve life's problems. Having lived in many states and traveled abroad, she was ready finally to settle into the farm life that her new husband offered her. While working as a farm wife, Diana was eventually diagnosed with bipolar disorder, a fact that she does not explore in this memoir. In between her numerous farm chores, she created a series of fabric art pieces that *show* what depression feels like. At the urging of her sister, she wrote a book about them. If you wish more information, feel free to check out her book, ***Depression Visible: The Ragged Edge***. If you have a depressive illness, know that you are not alone.

She uses her art and her book to educate people about depression and bipolar illnesses. "They can be treated," she says, "but the symptoms must be recognized as <u>symptoms</u>, not as lack of willpower or a character defect."

Diana is an artist. She is, as well, a farm wife (retired).

www.ingramcontent.com/pod-product-compliance
Lightning Source LLC
Chambersburg PA
CBHW081410270326
41931CB00016B/3438

9 781951 368463